SOVIET RUSSIA AND THE MIDDLE EAST

Studies in International Affairs Number 14

Studies in International Affairs Number 14

SOVIET RUSSIA AND THE MIDDLE EAST

by Aaron S. Klieman

The Washington Center of Foreign Policy Research
School of Advanced International Studies
The Johns Hopkins University

The Johns Hopkins Press, Baltimore and London

PREFACE

As the Russian silhouette spread across the Middle East at the close of the last decade, events have tended to substantiate my central thesis. A strong position in the Arab world has become of primary importance for Soviet strategic, economic, and foreign policies, and it will be safeguarded, even at great cost, whether against Israel, the United States and the West, or the Arabs themselves. Moscow's resolve was confirmed by the decision in March of this year to support Egypt with more sophisticated aircraft and missiles and to station air combat officers there, despite the inherent risk of clashing with Israel and forcing Washington to intervene on the latter's behalf. The battle on and for the Suez Canal has begun.

Several developments suffice to highlight the interplay between regional and global forces presently at work in Middle Eastern affairs. Arab fears of subservience to the Kremlin are finally being voiced and, what is no less important, by such revolutionary Arab leaders as Algeria's Houri Boumedienne and Libya's Muammar Ghaddafi. The unexpected election victory by the Conservative Party holds the prospect of a more active British role east of Suez. President Nasser's visit to Moscow at the end of June indicates greater coordination between the two uncomfortable allies. Continuing paralysis of the United Nations, the slow pace of great power conversations on this troubled area, and the general lack of enthusiasm for the latest American peace offensives cast doubts as to prospects for any imminent resolution of the Arab-Israeli conflict. At the same time, daily fighting between the combatants and the almost weekly friction between Arab governments and Palestinian organizations ensure unabating tension.

It is this complicated interplay, stemming in part from Soviet activism throughout the region, which raises the specter of the superpowers, and hence the international community—even despite their calculations and best intentions—entering on a collision course in the Middle East.

A.S.K.
Chicago

July 5, 1970

CONTENTS

SOVIET RUSSIA AND
THE MIDDLE EAST

Studies in International Affairs Number 14

I. INTRODUCTION

Long before the inception of the Cold War, Turkey, Iran, and Afghanistan constituted the first line of defense against the threat of Russian expansion southward into Asia. These countries—or, as John Foster Dulles named them, the "northern tier"—were drawn into a comprehensive system of containment inspired and bolstered by the western powers. Sharing nearly 2,700 miles of frontier with Soviet Russia and a common historical fear of its territorial ambitions, they represented a strong central link between Europe and the Far East in what soon became a global confrontation with communism. The tangible presence of the U.S. Sixth Fleet in Mediterranean waters and the lingering primacy of the British Royal Navy in the Persian Gulf reinforced both the Turks and Iranians in their steadfastness. The northern tier proved its durability as a politico-strategic concept in the Near and Middle East for at least the first fifteen years of the Cold War.

Since the early 1960s, however, this defensive wall has become porous, if not vestigial, in the face of a renewed Soviet effort at penetration, eschewing bluntness in favor of greater diplomatic subtlety and political adroitness. Turkey, Iran, and Afghanistan have been receptive to Moscow's conciliatory gestures, finding the Soviet policy of good neighborliness both refreshing and advantageous. The Kremlin leadership, encouraged by this receptivity and by other opportunities that exist in contemporary international relations, gradually has been implementing two foreign policy objectives, both of which originate in traditional Russian aspirations.

The Soviet Union has emerged recently as a formidable sea power of global dimensions. In addition, it has succeeded in acquiring a tangible presence in the strategic nexus of the eastern Mediterranean, a region held in high regard for centuries by Russian statesmen. This dual initiative is best symbolized by the Soviet naval squadron permanently on station in the Mediterranean Sea. By literally circumnavigating the northern tier land barrier, the Russians, in effect, have frustrated the western Cold War strategy of containment. In the process, they have gained influence in a number of Arab countries, have helped to solidify revolutionary regimes from Algeria to Iraq, and have secured the status of a full participant in Middle Eastern affairs, as evidenced by their prominent role during the Lebanese crisis at the end of 1969 and by their involvement in all efforts at a great power accord on the Arab-Israeli conflict.

Repercussions also may be traced to regions seemingly far removed from the Mediterranean and the Middle East. For the first time the Soviets have immediate access to, and the potential for control of, the adjacent sea lanes: the Red Sea, the Persian Gulf, and the Arabian Sea; the South Atlantic Ocean and the Indian Ocean; and, ultimately, the China Seas in the Far East. Such maritime access carries with it the prospect of intensified political activity not only in the eastern Mediterranean, but in Arabia, Africa, the Indian subcontinent, and Southeast Asia as well. Direct influence in the Arab Middle East and the maneuverability afforded by sea power, if fully developed and exploited in concert, can be expected to determine global configurations of power during the coming decade.

A striking feature of the Soviet initiative is its timeliness, for Moscow has been the beneficiary of circumstances facilitating its penetration into the seas and countries of the Third World. Britain, which served as the principal deterrent to Russian expansion during its reign of four centuries as "monarch of the seas" and guardian over the main approach routes to the British Empire, is in the final process of liquidating imperial holdings and obligations east of Suez. In addition, the United States, which succeeded Britain in 1945 as the foremost naval power, gives evidence of late of serious reservations in accepting and, even more, of perpetuating such a role.

Uncertainty of purpose within the western alliance system has been another circumstance operating in favor of Soviet success. An era opened in which the rationale for existing collective alliances was subjected to fundamental review. NATO, since its inception, has been oriented toward the European continent and the threat posed by the Red Army. Hence its heightened interest with Soviet naval activity in the Mediterranean even now is concerned with implications for the southern flank of Europe rather than for the western extremity of Asia.[1] CENTO and SEATO have also experienced centrifugal pressures likely to prevent any multilateral assumption of responsibility for insuring against foreign encroachment either by land or by sea. Indeed, the very instability of the former colonial holdings has been advantageous for Soviet purposes. The developing nations in general, and those of the Middle East in particular, lack the strength to police their own waters or to guarantee the impermeability of their territorial boundaries. Their compelling economic needs, their propensity for discerning the animus of imperialism behind every gesture and action by the West, and the intensity of intraregional rivalries will continue to present the Soviet Union with additional opportunities for extending its transoceanic influence.

In 1963, President Kennedy noted political changes taking place in the Middle East, "which still do not show a precise pattern." While the question of precision is always open to subjective interpretation, the prominence of Soviet Russia as a sea power with extensive political interests in and beyond the Arab world has become increasingly apparent by 1970. Soviet naval mobility already represents a substantial increment in communist power and prestige, but at heavy cost to the domestic economy and in the face of uncertainty regarding their political influence, which may prove to be as much a liability as an asset. While clarity doubtless will be provided in the natural course of events, it is possible in the interim to trace the evolution of the Soviet strategic and political initiative along the eastern shores of the Mediterranean and south of the northern tier countries. This study recalls the historical antecedents of Russian concern for this region, describes the uncertain status of the Middle East today, and relates both of these to the latest Soviet attempts at ascendancy. It is intended to be a purposeful meditation and analysis before, rather than after, Russian power in the Persian Gulf and east of Suez becomes a fait accompli. As a student of the region, Sir John A. R. Marriott, cautioned more than fifty year ago:

> The Balkans, Egypt, Mesopotamia are again today, what from the dawn of history they have been, objects of jealous desire to all economically minded peoples. Less from the point of view of occupation than of control; less for their intrinsic importance than as a means of access to other lands. Hence the concentration of international rivalries upon the lands which fringe the Eastern Mediterranean. That rivalry has not exhausted itself during the last twenty centuries; on the contrary, it seems possible that we may be about to witness its manifestation on a scale without precedent in the history of the world.[2]

The Soviet Union has opened a new phase of the persistent struggle for power in the Middle East known to an earlier generation of historians, diplomats, and generals as the Eastern Question.

I. THE ARAB MIDDLE EAST IN WORLD POLITICS

Great diversity is the most readily apparent characteristic of the post imperial Middle East; it is also a major cause of instability in the area. Geopolitical centrality in the past had been both a primary asset for the Middle East and a source of extreme vulnerability. Because events of the last twenty-five years have tended to strengthen the heterogeneity from within and the convergence of strategic interests from without, these two characteristics still help to explain why the contemporary Middle East is an unstable region which is prejudicing international peace and encouraging superpower competition.

This quality of diversity is initially perceived on the physical plane of climate, topography, and vegetation. It extends as well to the peoples of the area, who have distinct historical experiences, cultures, social outlook, and political orientation. Economic disparities are a major factor in regional affairs. An uneven distribution of wealth, particularly the location of oil deposits, finds those states most directly involved in the confrontation with Israel—namely, Egypt, Jordan, and Syria—financially dependent upon the conservative oil states. However, Saudi Arabia, Kuwait, and, until recently, Libya are less disposed to fund domestic revolution and less preoccupied with destroying Israel, both of which have increased Russia's prominence in the area. Such a high degree of variegation, which gave rise to the term "levantinism," while appealing to the western romantic, scholar, or traveler, has exasperated imperialist proconsuls and native rulers alike. It is operative on both an intrastate and interstate basis, creating friction and conflict within them and among them. Domestic instability and interstate rivalries act in turn to encourage intervention by outside powers, unilaterally or collectively, either for maximum individual gain or for the minimal objective of perpetuating the status quo.

An analogous situation is offered by the parochialism which attended the Holy Roman Empire's demise and the divisions within Christendom. Tension between the disruptive pressure of narrow loyalties, on the one hand, and a nostalgic quest for reunification, on the other, have provided a major theme of European history. In the case of the Middle East, the extension of the continental state system to the eastern shores of the Mediterranean after the First World War introduced new lines of cleavage. The Anglo–French partition of the Ottoman Empire encouraged political entities and loyalties previously nonexistent. The very fact that local patriotism has taken root to the extent it has in fifty years is testimony to the impact of western nationalism. Yet the Arabs, too, retain a longing for that cohesion which disintegrated along with the Muslim caliphate after the thirteenth century—a longing given modern expression in the idea and movements on behalf of Arab unity. Napoleon and France, who in the nineteenth century sought to restore a semblance of unity to Europe through hegemony, find their Middle Eastern counterparts today in Nasser and Egypt. Whereas the European nations, in their interlocking rivalries, earlier sought ascendancy through overseas possessions, these latter territories, now grown to statehood, have reversed the process: Their security, or at least a measure of it, is found in the economic and diplomatic patronage of outside powers. In the case of the Arab countries, the Soviet Union has been wooed in the past decade more than any other outside power.

Regional heterogeneity also has had the effect of frustrating efforts at any single accepted delineation of the territorial scope of the Middle East, despite the penchant of geographers and social scientists for neat compartmentalization. Recourse to the original application of the term "Middle East," however, may offer some meaning and coherence, as well as an insight into the strategic value of this region from the Russian perspective.

During the nineteenth century, the land beginning at the eastern edge of the Mediterranean was viewed by the British in terms of its value for the far-flung British Empire. It was considered, above all, as a strategic medium because of the network of waterways offering alternate corridors to India. The Mediterranean Sea linked Europe with Asia, and the Red Sea and the Persian Gulf were the terminals for two overland routes to India via Egypt and Mesopotamia. As early as 1826 the *Bombay Courier* observed, ". . . it is hardly possible to look at a map of the world without receiving a kind of impression that nature, in her physical operations, had intended those two seas [the Mediterranean and the Red Sea] to facilitate the communication between Europe, Asia, and Africa, and left it to the enterprise and ingenuity of man to take advantage of her arrangements."[1] Human enterprise and ingenuity produced the Suez Canal. When opened in 1869, it afforded European commerce a short, all-water route to the Orient and reinforced the maritime frame of reference toward the Near East.

In 1902 an American naval historian, Alfred Thayer Mahan, first employed the term "Middle East" in discussing the vast area between Arabia and India centering upon the Persian Gulf. Official British endorsement was given to this usage in 1921 when a Middle East

Department was established under Colonial Office auspices to administer the mandates for Mesopotamia and Palestine and to govern relations with the several rulers of Arabia.

The reassuring presence of the Royal Navy came to be taken for granted in the interwar period, and attention shifted to the land itself, with emphasis on individual countries. Attempts to extract narrower similarities from the midst of regional diversity have resulted oftentimes in political distortion and terminological ambiguity. Either certain regional segments and traits are analyzed to the exclusion of others, or artificial entities are created for the sake of convenience. Consequently, one finds frequent mention of such terms as the "northern tier," "the Fertile Crescent," and the "Maghrib" states of North Africa, though such entities do not conform to reality. They have been coined and imposed from outside, lack institutionalization, and have yet to produce any sort of identification on the part of the local inhabitants residing within them. The Red Sea is taken to be the southern extremity of the Middle East, despite its having been the medium for considerable interaction culturally and historically between Africa and Asia.

Reapplication of the original naval reference would make the region an open one, serving to integrate rather than to isolate other areas. Accordingly, the Middle East today is that area bounded by the Black Sea, the eastern Mediterranean, the Red Sea, the Arabian Sea, and the Persian Gulf. In terms of specific countries, it directly includes Turkey, Iraq, Syria, Lebanon, Jordan, Israel, Egypt, the Persian Gulf sheikhdoms, Saudi Arabia, Kuwait, Yemen, and Southern Yemen (known as Aden before its independence in November, 1967).

These five bodies of water, when conceived of as

bridges rather than barriers to political interaction, indirectly affect neighboring riparian countries: the Soviet Union to the north; the North African states of Morocco, Tunisia, Algeria, and Libya; Sudan and the countries along the Horn of Africa to the south; and, finally, Iran and the Indian subcontinent to the east. The heightened interest of the Soviet Union in these waters, their littorals, and narrow passageways aids in reinforcing this maritime perspective on the Middle East.

The Middle East, as a political actor in world affairs, was conveniently restrained for long periods. First under Turkish and then under British and French domination, its centrifugal forces were suppressed and its waterways were effectively controlled. National independence in the years before and after the Second World War marked the Middle East's transition from a passive arena of international rivalries to the status of an actor as well. But in addition to creating entirely new problems, such as the compatibility of Arab unity with the existence of sovereign states, independence has forced many of the latent domestic and regional tensions to the surface once again. The region is politically fragmented, inherently unstable, and suffers from what Jacques Berque has termed "the disruption of traditional man."

Ordinarily one could assume that the tensions within the Middle East would be an adequate deterrent against involvement by external powers, especially in light of Britain's debilitating experience in this region at a less complicated time in history. Yet both the United States and the Soviet Union have been less prudent than opportunistic at crucial moments in the past two decades. They have undertaken commitments and cast themselves deeper into Middle Eastern affairs, despite the region's inherent instability. As a result, the Middle

East by the end of the 1960s once again had become an arena, perhaps even the salient one, of great power competition.

Immediately after the Second World War, Stalin made a bold bid for a foothold in the Middle East. He asked Turkey to cede two northern provinces and sought the right to garrison the Turkish Straits. He plotted to set up a puppet government in Azerbaijan, Iran, and demanded oil concessions. He even strove to obtain control over one of the former Italian colonies in North Africa. Frustrated in all three efforts by the combined opposition of the Turks, Iranians, British, and Americans, he tried to make political capital from the British predicament in Palestine by endorsing the U.N. partition plan in November, 1947, and then extending to Israel full diplomatic recognition in May, 1948. The coolness which developed in Soviet-Israeli relations by 1951 ended the first phase of Soviet postwar interest in the Middle East. It had been marked by a series of political failures and ideological disillusionment with the small, factious, and ineffectual local communist parties. It was in this period, 1945–51, that the strategic balance swung even more in Russia's disfavor because of the appearance of the U.S. Sixth Fleet as a permanent, tangible symbol of western resolve to exclude Soviet influence from the Middle East.

The turning point, however, came in 1955, when Stalin's successors sanctioned an arms agreement between Czechoslovakia and the revolutionary government which had seized power in Egypt in July, 1952. The Kremlin, mindful of past shortcomings, eagerly seized upon Egypt's estrangement from the West over the two issues of the Suez Canal and the Aswan Dam. It assumed the position formerly held by Britain and the United States as munitions supplier and financier to the Egyptian government, and cultivated that personal relationship with Gamal Abdul Nasser which has remained a constant of Soviet policy through the 1960s.

Their singular success in Egypt notwithstanding, the Soviets continued to foster new client relationships which often proved futile and embarrassing. Moscow initially counted on Abdul Karim Kassim, co-executor of the 1958 revolution in Iraq, as a willing ally. Once he began restricting activities of the local communist party and challenging President Nasser's growing regional influence, the Soviets quickly lost their enthusiasm. They also overestimated the ability of the republican regime in Yemen to suppress the loyalist opposition, even with Egyptian military assistance, after September, 1962. By 1969 greater attention was being shown instead toward the Peoples' Republic of Southern Yemen, sovereign over the key port city of Aden.

In May, 1967, the Soviet Union was placed in an uncomfortable position by the extremism of their protégés in Syria. Their unwillingness or inability to serve as a moderating influence became an important factor in precipitating the Six Day War the following month. Such a propensity for involvement in an inherently unstable region was epitomized in the months following the 1967 crisis, for at that point the Soviets at least had the option of disengaging themselves politically if not economically. The patent failure of the Arab armies to even maintain a credible defense certainly offered an understandable justification and a fitting occasion. Instead, the Soviets proceeded to broaden their commitments to the Arab cause and to deepen their investment in President Nasser, the United Arab Republic, and the growing number of revolutionary regimes in the area.

Thus, since 1945 the Soviet Union has undergone a long process of adapting itself to the temper of the Arab world. Above and beyond all the fluctuations in its policy and fortunes, three significant trends may be distinguished in terms of focus, emphasis, and rationale. First, the Soviets—who were unable to achieve their objectives in the Middle East through the Turks, Persians, or even the Israelis—have elected to concentrate instead on the "southern tier" of the Arab countries. The fact that this approach has been succeeding may have induced both Ankara and Tehran more recently, as acts of prudence, to mend their fences with Moscow.

Second, the emphasis in Soviet policy has been shifted increasingly from ideological considerations to strategic motives. Whereas in the early postwar years the Soviet leaders worked primarily through local Arab communist parties, they have felt little compunction, when circumstances have dictated, about having closer ties with such reactionary, bourgeois regimes as the Jordanian monarchy, or with Egypt, whose native communists have long been circumscribed and imprisoned.

Third, Soviet policy toward the Arabs does not appear to conform with the traditional theory of alliances. Rather than valuing the Arabs for any positive contribution or singular strength—military, for example—they might bring to an alliance relationship, it is more likely the very fact of their weakness which has induced Soviet support on such a large scale. Arab political instability, social contradictions, economic deficiencies, and military vulnerability have been exploited by the Soviet Union to secure a wide range of objectives, of which strategic mobility is certainly among the most prominent. Access to the several major ports and naval bases of the Middle East may in itself warrant the expenditure of military supplies, industrial equipment, and diplomatic activity on the Arabs' behalf.

The period since 1945 has also been one of increased

involvement by the United States in the Middle East, too. So brief was the transition from world war to Cold War that it prevented any calm reassessment of priorities by Washington. The containment of communism proceeded without any clearly defined guidelines for policy, certainly with regard to the Arabs. Another weakness stemmed from the negative aspects of the hyphenated Anglo-American relationship. Arab contempt for England, the West, and its political institutions began to surface in the 1930s; this was gradually extended to encompass the United States through guilt by association.[2] In short, while the Soviet Union has had to overcome its own ideological rigidity and the predatory image of its past, the United States is still struggling, with little success, to divorce itself from the imperialist record of its closest European allies.

Circumstances between 1945 and 1950 did not favor an American decision to avoid responsibilities in the eastern Mediterranean. As soon as the German threat to the Balkans and North Africa had been averted, a new threat was perceived in the form of Soviet encroachment. As British resolve weakened, the United States found itself assuming a greater portion of the fivefold burden: protecting the sources of oil vital for European reconstruction; arbitrating the complex Palestine problem; countering any Soviet thrust southward; ensuring free navigation; and guaranteeing the sovereignty of regional states. Toward the close of the 1960s, Britain announced its intention to terminate comparable responsibilities east of Suez. By this time, however, the United States had shown far less enthusiasm for filling the expected vacuum once again.

The Truman Doctrine of 1947, prompted by Soviet efforts at subverting Greece and Turkey, expressed American acceptance of the challenge to lead the defense of western interests in the Mediterranean. Originally limited in scope, the U.S. commitment widened to incorporate those Arab states willing to participate in a more comprehensive military arrangement designed implicitly to contain the Soviet Union. In 1950 the American government accepted responsibility jointly with Britain and France in regulating the flow of arms into the Middle East.

The next attempt at organizing the Arab states on behalf of larger western strategic considerations came in 1955, when the Baghdad Pact was signed by Iran, Iraq, Pakistan, Turkey, and Great Britain. It was hoped that through the medium of Iraq the northern tier countries could be linked with the Arab states to form a strong security system; this, in turn, would be "an integral part of the peace and security of all the nations of the world." The Baghdad Pact, however, proved an abject failure. Rather than accepting direct membership, the United States contented itself with reaffirming its support for the collective efforts of these nations and with warning that a threat to the territorial integrity or political independence of the Baghdad Pact members would be viewed "with the utmost gravity." Anglo-American differences emerged over objectives and means as well as over respective roles. By stressing the interrelated defenses of the northern countries and the southern Arab tier, the western powers overlooked the major differences in outlook and priorities between the two regions. The *coup de grace* against the Baghdad Pact was delivered by the Arab states. Activated for the first time by Nasser, they refused to emulate Iraq in joining the western camp. In 1957, through the Eisenhower Doctrine, Washington abandoned the guise of Anglo–American solidarity by unilaterally proffering support to any Middle Eastern state exposed to Soviet-sponsored aggression or infiltration. Only Lebanon in 1958 availed itself of this offer, and even then reluctantly.

The Suez crisis in 1956 highlighted the weaknesses of American policy. The United States sought at last to adopt an independent course, refusing to endorse the use of force by its allies, England and France, against Egypt; but it was still unable to establish a meaningful relationship with the Arab nationalist movement, Egypt in particular.[3] Casting about for some operational framework, the United States took recourse in the same policy that had backfired for the British. It found greater compatibility and consistency in the Arab monarchs and conservative leaders in Jordan, Lebanon, Libya, Morocco, Saudi Arabia, Kuwait, and Tunisia. Yet the history of the area since 1950 quite clearly did not auger well for these forms of government, beginning with the bloodless deposition of the Egyptian monarchy in 1952 and the more violent overthrow of the Iraqi and Yemeni rulers in 1958 and 1962. Nor does the trend give evidence of abating, as indicated by the coups which occurred in rapid succession in the Sudan and Libya in 1969, and the tenuous position of the pro-western governments in Jordan and Lebanon.

Both superpowers, despite their past rebuffs and political setbacks at the hands of unpredictable Arab regimes, began the 1970s with commitments in the Middle East. Soviet policy in recent years has moved in the direction of incurring further responsibilities, whereas American interest during the same period declined significantly, partially by choice but also of necessity due to Arab enmity. The current Soviet initiative, however, works to prevent America's complete isolation from events in that region.

One explanation for this shared predisposition toward involvement in the Middle East derives from the nature of current world politics, governed by a complex of normative rules and restraints which have resulted from twenty-five years of Cold War diplomacy. An abiding equilibrium has come to prevail in Europe; this was marked by the tacit mutual acceptance of its being divided de facto between East and West. Hopes for a détente were centered primarily on Europe, encouraged by the policy of West Germany to ease relations with Poland and East Germany. The Czechoslovak experience of 1968 vividly illustrated Soviet determination to prevent any diminution of its sphere of influence in Eastern Europe. The Brezhnev Doctrine confirmed this in terms of the Marxist dialectic, justifying the use of force because "the weakening of any of the links in the world system of socialism directly affects all the socialist countries, which cannot look indifferently upon this."[4]

The attitude of the United States toward Latin America, one of proprietary interest, is still derived from the Monroe Doctrine established in the early part of the nineteenth century. Castro's Cuba has been effectively isolated; as an irritant for the United States it is somewhat analogous to West Berlin within the confines of Eastern Europe. Consequently, American preeminence in the Western Hemisphere, though of dubious prestige value at times, is not seriously challenged from without.

This stabilization of power, however, has not been extended to Asia, Africa, or the Middle East. In Asia, the United States and the Soviet Union, with confirmed spheres of their own elsewhere, have been reluctant to bestow a comparable privilege upon Communist China. With respect to the African continent, neither superpower had participated in its partition by Europe, and therefore lacked any established interests to defend.

The case of the Middle East was quite different, for both superpowers did have existing interests to preserve or to expand. Nor could they deny its strategic importance and the value of the Middle East's two outstanding assets: oil and water.

The overriding objectives of the superpowers are to consolidate what they already have achieved, to deny each other undue advantages in the three peripheral areas, and to avoid a direct confrontation.[5] The Middle East crisis of May–June, 1967, which supported hypotheses derived from the Cuban missile crisis, confirmed the affinity of interests and shared responsibilities of Washington and Moscow. Each appreciated that superpower and nuclear status carries with it the political, if not moral, imperative for crisis management in order to localize conflict. No less significant, each came to display greater sensitivity in perceiving its opponent's individual pressures and considerations.

Such stabilizing factors notwithstanding, the Cold War, in the Khrushchevian sense of peaceful coexistence, retains its saliency as the ordering principle of international relations. Precisely because of an approximate strategic balance between the United States and the Soviet Union, greater premium is given to probing for comparative advantage in peripheral areas as yet unincorporated into delineated spheres.

In somewhat different terms, the two global protagonists appreciate the implications of a balance of terror and of innovation in sophisticated weaponry proceeding without adequate safeguards. They respect each other's capacity for nuclear overkill and for the ability to protect their respective homelands from conventional military invasion. This awareness, together with the inordinate costs of the space race, weapons research, and maintenance of elaborate military establishments, has stimulated such joint efforts at accommodation as the Nuclear Test Ban Treaty and the strategic arms limitation talks. Similar efforts in the fields of arms control and disarmament, as well as in preventing the spread of nuclear weapons and prohibiting use of the ocean floor for military purposes, are either under way or being given serious consideration.

Competition in the peripheral areas of the Middle East, Africa, and Asia therefore becomes more attractive, whether in quest of an elusive security or in order to negotiate from a position of strength. This competition is also acceptable because it enables a superpower to expend comparatively small resources in gambling for a payoff in clients, influence, and prestige. Thereafter the difficulty lies in consolidating the gains and in preventing any erosion of power either through incompatibility with clients or more determined competition from the rival superpower.

A comparable situation of rigidity at the center of politics existed under the continental balance of power in Europe in the middle of the nineteenth century. And it was as a function of that particular stalemate that the scramble for an empire in Asia, Africa, and the Middle East took place, with the European powers seeking even marginal power increments beyond the actual confines of Europe.

It is in this context of the nineteenth-century precedent and the contemporary situation that the Middle East, with its instability, becomes prominent. It is a subordinate state system whose members still waver between socialism and capitalism, and it is the gateway to other target zones for competition in Africa and Asia. Consequently, it assumes an importance for the superpowers that far outweighs its liabilities.

A further dysfunctional element is Great Britain's recession from the Middle East, which was accelerated in 1947 by the withdrawal from India and Palestine. It took on greater momentum during the 1950s and the 1960s as the British failed to retain a presence in Egypt either through diplomacy or a show of force. Her Majesty's government was ejected unceremoniously from Jordan and Iraq; in 1967 it voluntarily relinquished control of Aden. The process is scheduled to end in 1971, when Britain will retract its presence in the Persian Gulf. Despite their investment and efforts, the British, with rare exceptions, have failed to leave behind stable successor governments. Their withdrawal has been neither prompt nor gracious enough to establish a legacy of goodwill toward, or trust in, the West. As a consequence, the Arab world is a vacuum open to the play of newer competitive forces and receptive to Soviet overtures.

Arab states within the region, of course, are all zealous in safeguarding their sovereignty, independence, and integrity. On their own, however, they are capable of little more than applying palliatives to domestic problems and of irritating disputes with neighboring countries. They therefore have proceeded to compromise themselves through dependence in one form or another upon the two global powers. And in establishing this relationship, they have contributed to converting the Third World into the primary arena of struggle between East and West.

The smaller powers often exploit the Cold War rivalry to obtain aid and armaments, and they do so without admitting they have incurred any commensurate obligations in return. It is difficult to accept, for example, that Egypt's position of neutrality has not been compromised, in spite of President Nasser's statement to Soviet officials: "All I do is ask, ask and ask, but you never ask for anything. What can I do for *you* for a change?"[6]

The number and types of Middle Eastern disputes, both existing and potential, are enough to tax the patience of contingency planners and weaken the enthusiasm of foreign affairs experts. Strains within each polity are one major source of disequilibrium, producing a sequence of political intrigues, coups, and revolutions. In Syria and Iraq, this spiral has become a fact of social and political life. In Yemen, a partially successful, or unconsolidated, coup led to open civil war after 1962 and to outside intervention by Egypt and Saudi Arabia. Other principal causes for internal unrest are competition within the military elite (e.g., in Iraq) and factionalism over ideological issues (e.g., in the Ba'ath Party). Ethnic separateness is an enduring problem for Lebanon, with its Christian and Muslim communities. The same holds true for Iraq, divided into Shia and Sunni Muslim sects, and for Sudan, with its black African population in the south alienated from the Muslim center of power at Khartoum.

Rivalry for regional primacy and for leadership of the Arab renaissance continues to plague relations between Egypt, Syria, Iraq, and Saudi Arabia. Traditional animosities, such as Arab against Turk and Muslim against Christian, provide an undercurrent of tension enveloping the entire region. Equally significant are sectarian differences between countries, most notably Shiite Iran versus Sunni Iraq. Ethiopia's prospects of surviving as a Christian monarchy having access to the Red Sea are lessened by the existence of revolutionary Muslim regimes in neighboring Sudan and Somalia and by a militant secessionist movement in the Muslim province of Eritrea. The lingering influence of religion in intraregional politics in this secular age was confirmed by the Muslim conference at Rabat in 1969, following the damage to Jerusalem's al-Aksa mosque, at which India, a Hindu country with a large Muslim minority, was effectively isolated by Pakistan.

Dynastic feuds, a major irritant in inter-Arab relations in previous decades, have virtually disappeared, except for slight traces between Hashimite Jordan and Saudi Arabia. The rulers have found a greater common cause in merely surviving. The problem of traditional feuds, however, has been replaced by that of personal ambitions of individual rulers. Irredentism and territorial claims at one time or another during the 1960s poisoned relations between the following nations: Iran and Bahrein; Iraq and Kuwait; Morocco and Algeria; and Iran and Iraq over the Shatt al-Arab outlet to the Persian Gulf. Late in 1969, fighting between Saudi Arabia and Southern Yemen over possession of an obscure desert outpost added to the growing list of regional animosities. Because none of these claims has been either resolved amicably or renounced, they are likely to become sources for crises in the future. Other ominous problems include the frustrated nationalism of the Kurds and the question of succession, which was resolved in Libya by the deposition of King Idris, but which takes on increasing importance for Saudi Arabia, Tunisia, Jordan, Ethiopia, and even for Egypt. In addition, the determination of the Trucial sheikhdoms' political future will affect all the other Persian Gulf states.

The emergence of the Palestinian liberation movement after 1967 introduces a new ingredient of uncertainty and instability to the Middle East. Since 1939, when Britain for the first time invited the several Arab countries to participate in discussions on Palestine's future, the Palestinians have been spoken for by outsiders, who invariably approach the subject largely on the basis of self-interest. The activist groups provide one positive function, that of returning the Palestine problem to its original dimension as a clash between Jewish nationalism and Palestinian Arab nationalism. However, the components of the nascent movement have shown a definite proclivity for struggling as much among themselves and with their host Arab countries as against Israel. The raids on Israel by *al-Fatah* from bases in Jordan and Lebanon have caused Israel to retaliate against those two countries. The movement has thus compromised both host governments, and it is behind the crisis atmosphere which has prevailed in Lebanon since October, 1969. The negotiations conducted at Cairo to end that particular crisis confirmed the central role of *al-Fatah's* Yasir Arafat by satisfying his demands for greater latitude in launching raids against Israel from Lebanese soil. His success in dictating terms by the threat of force, in compromising Lebanese sovereignty, and in challenging established authorities can only be viewed by other Arab governments as an ominous precedent. In a similar vein, the liberation movement favors forcing Israel to retaliate and to occupy additional Arab territory. This is hardly a cause for rejoicing in Egypt, Jordan, or Syria, which lost substantial territories in 1967.

The Arab dispute with Israel in general has received perhaps too much prominence in the analysis of contemporary Middle Eastern affairs. One unfortunate result is the political subordination and scholarly neglect of the tensions mentioned above, which are no less prejudicial to peace. Closer examination of the Middle East in all of its complexity should caution that resolution of this one specific problem would by no means guarantee the peace and stability desired by American presidents and statesmen. Nor would it effectively isolate the region from great power influence. Indeed, in the extreme case of the dissolution of Israel, the Palestine problem merely would complicate matters by raising once again the inter-Arab question of who gets what territory in the division of spoils.

Scarcely any diplomatic initiative has been forthcoming, either from within the region or by outside agencies, to resolve the manifold regional problems or disputes. The series of discussions between the United States and the Soviet Union which began in 1968, and which were expanded at times to include France and Great Britain, must be seen as belated. Western pressure might have been effective in the formative stages of the Arab-Israeli dispute, but three major clashes in the last twenty years have hardened the rival positions into intransigence. Since 1948 the Arab leaders have subordinated internal priorities to the single issue of challenging Israel's existence. Nevertheless, it is as superficial to equate the Arab-Israeli conflict with regional instability as it is a disservice to all the peoples of the area, who have pressing economic and social needs.

The Arab Summit Conference at Rabat in December, 1969, illustrated once again the serious underlying problems which persist in dividing the Arab world. President Nasser had urged the conference in order to determine a unified approach against Israel; instead, the conference was reduced to a forum for airing individual and national grievances. The delegates split along conservative and revolutionary lines which seemed to presage renewed conflict between the two factions in coming years. President Nasser, who had hoped to devise a detailed mobilization plan with a more equitable distribution of resources and responsibilities, was caught in the middle. Faced by resistance on all sides, he suffered still another blow to his leadership in the Arab Middle East.

In view of these discomforting elements, what advantages would control of the Middle East bring to either superpower? Surely dominance over this vast area of diversity would necessitate playing the role of arbiter and coping with the inherent tensions. Much of the answer lies in the fact that this region, more than any other from the contemporary global perspective, has a commanding geopolitical position.

Until the nineteenth century the lands washed by the eastern Mediterranean were of little immediate or intrinsic value to Europe. Harbors in the region facilitated commerce, its inhabitants offered a market for goods and ideas, and its religious sites, recalling the birthplaces of Christianity, Judaism, and Islam, appealed to pilgrims. Still it lacked any single outstanding natural resource, being equated in the European mind with desert, camel caravans, and nomadic bedouin. The discovery of oil and its application to industrial production, travel, and military technology drastically increased the value of the region. By 1967 the Middle East was producing almost 28 percent of the world's output of crude oil, with 62.8 percent of proven oil reserves located in the Arabian peninsula alone. For nearly one hundred years the Suez Canal, which functioned as the major east-west transit route, also enhanced the region's value. In 1966, the last full year of uninterrupted passage, the Suez Canal handled 21,250 vessels with a total of 274.3 million tons.

The Suez Canal emphasized the special attraction of the Middle East: being "the hub of the Eastern Hemisphere," it could be used as the means to other ends. Even in ancient times it had been the channel for intercultural penetration between East and West. Within a global context, the Middle East gives unlimited commercial and strategic mobility. Its internal sea lanes, land routes, and air corridors form a transportation grid linking Europe with the unexploited Asian and African continents.

In time of war, control of these routes, offering maneuverability, might prove to be a decisive advantage. In time of peace, when there is greater emphasis on foreign transactions, such control would enable a major industrial nation to secure valuable outlets for trade. During a period of protracted great power rivalry short of war, such as at present, control of this grid enables any nation to demonstrate the credibility of its power before any ally, antagonist, or neutral party. Superpower status implies, no less than thermonuclear strength, an ability to affect events and decisions in any part of the globe, however remote. The Soviet Union, in particular, has suffered from this deficiency in the past. One central motive for the Kremlin's exploitation of recent turbulence in the Middle East is a desire to redress this shortcoming while the opportunity exists.

The Middle East was regarded as merely a sideshow during the two world wars of this century, when the major theaters of combat were in Europe and Asia. By their words and actions during the latest phase of the Cold War, Soviet Russia and, to a lesser extent, France are underlining once again the central importance of the Middle East in world politics. The region will be appreciated, as always, for its intrinsic value, such as the rich oil reserves to be found there. But it will be coveted even more for the political, commercial, and strategic opportunities available beyond its immediate perimeter in Europe, Asia, and Africa. The late John Foster Dulles perhaps put the region into its proper international perspective. Following his visit there in 1953, Dulles emphasized the need for more attention by the United States to the problems and conditions in the Near East and South Asia, because "that area was and is very important, but not all-important." The Middle East still is not all-important; but neither have there been any developments making it any less important than in 1953.

The geopolitical importance of the Middle East was well understood in London during the nineteenth and twentieth centuries. Because of physical contiguity, this conception was appreciated even earlier in Moscow; to the tsars, this region was *Blizhnii Vostok,* the *near* East. It has only been reinforced through a long record of frustration at the hands of the British. In order to understand some of the motives for, and implications of, the current Soviet effort it is necessary therefore to inquire into the historical patterns of Russia's relationship to the Middle East.

I. RUSSIA AND THE MIDDLE EAST: A HISTORICAL PERSPECTIVE

Geographic proximity makes Russia susceptible to those forces which attract imperial nations to the Middle East and the Mediterranean Sea basin. The centrality of the eastern Mediterranean in Russian strategic thought and national interests is reflected in diplomatic history covering the two hundred years since Russia first gained entry to that sea in 1770, committing itself thereafter to the persisting struggle for its mastery.

The Russians' interest in the Mediterranean has been traced to the original landlocked condition of Muscovite Russia, which urged them toward the sea. Almost from the moment political unity was achieved and economic potentialities were grasped, the question of the Black Sea, of free movement on its waters, and of unobstructed egress through the Dardanelles became a preoccupation of tsarist statecraft. Peter the Great gave impetus to this drive before his death in 1725, advancing to the Sea of Azov and enjoining his countrymen to press on toward Constantinople and India. Utilization of the navy to fulfill a perceived national destiny became part of the tsarist legacy inherited by the Bolsheviks, though they did not subscribe to it until the 1960s.

By the eighteenth century, Russia had explored all of the alternatives for access to the sea. It reached its natural western extremity at the Baltic, establishing St. Petersburg as a window onto Europe. However, ports fronting on the Baltic, such as Kronshtadt, were blocked by ice, so that any maritime activity had to be confined to a few select months of each year. The second alternative, the Pacific, could only be reached by pushing across the vastness of Central Asia. Russia did persist in this direction, nevertheless, and achieved great power status in the Far East when, in 1860, China ceded territory between the Ussuri River and the Pacific Ocean. Though Vladivostok became Russia's Pacific naval base in 1872, it still had to be provisioned from Moscow along 5,700 miles of the Trans-Siberian railroad.

These basically unalterable conditions of climate and topography inevitably led Peter's successors to focus on the remaining alternative of the Azov-Black Sea-Mediterranean route, which offered warm-water ports open year-round and conveniently located near the centers of production. This route necessitated direct confrontation with the Ottoman Empire, which regulated transit through the Dardanelles. But unlike the obstacles imposed by nature, this impediment could be overcome through human effort and political pressure.

In 1768, Catherine the Great involved Russia in another in a series of direct assaults against the Ottoman Empire. At one point in this war the Russian fleet played an ephemeral yet significant role in Mediterranean affairs: After an arduous journey around Europe, it passed Gibraltar and destroyed the Turkish naval forces in the battle of Tchesma. Partially as a result of this naval presence, Russia gained recognition as a Black Sea power by the treaty of Kutchuk Kaynardji in 1774. This treaty stirred ambitions for outright control of the Turkish Straits, and it extended Russian horizons to the Mediterranean. It also provided a theme for Russian-Ottoman relations which endured until the demise of the empires during the First World War. Because the Turks remained in Constantinople and hence in control of the Black Sea-Mediterranean passage, this was the farthest advance in the direction of the Mediterranean that tsarist statesmen and admirals were able to make.

Conceivably, Russia might have persevered against the Ottoman Empire had the rivalry been localized between the two regional powers. Instead, Great Britain intervened, repeatedly and decisively, on behalf of a Near Eastern balance of power, which meant the defense of Turkish territorial integrity. Britain's ability to confine Russia to the Black Sea was a function largely of naval supremacy in the eastern Mediterranean. Its proprietary claim to dominance had been registered well before the end of the eighteenth century, while Russia was still busy securing its position in the Black Sea. The mercantile system, the continental power struggle, and imperial dictates in India prompted successive stages of Britain's extension of interests and control from the western to the eastern periphery of the Mediterranean, symbolized by the line of elaborate palisades and naval bases beginning at Gibraltar, which has been under the British flag since 1704.

Calculations of self-interest and of international responsibilities—their differentiation often being elusive—thus worked to ensure that Britain would actively support the existence of the Ottoman Empire and its retention of control over the Straits in defiance of Russian counterclaims. Distinctive imperial orientations between Russia and Britain resulted from this impasse. The former, whenever checked at the Straits, had little choice but to return to the status dictated for it by geopolitical realities, that of a continental land power. The latter, meanwhile, established itself as the leading sea power by 1588. Russia, when seeking territorial aggrandizement, had to look either to Central Europe and the Balkans or to China and Japan in Asia. Britain, on the other hand, because of its naval strength, could administer a large and widely dispersed empire, and it had the capacity to intervene at virtually any point on the globe.

These specializations were demonstrated in the contribution each made to the defeat of a common enemy, Napoleonic France. By withdrawing further into the Russian heartland, Alexander I destroyed the French army in 1812. The British, in turn, defeated the French navy off the coast of Egypt in 1798, and again at Trafalgar in 1805. Still, due to the naval *cordon sanitaire* directed against it in particular, the Russian national psychology developed certain negative traits: frustration, fear of encirclement, and preoccupation with a search for security.

After the defeat of Napoleon, Russia emerged once again as the foremost threat to Ottoman survival and British primacy. The nineteenth century, with its progression of military campaigns and peace treaties and the constant threat of renewed hostilities, serves to depict the intensity and futility of Russian efforts at altering the Mediterranean balance.[1] Tsarist policy toward the Eastern Question in the period from the Congress of Vienna to Sarajevo oscillated between six basic options: suasion, negotiation, amity, introspection, belligerence, and diversion.

Dissolution of the Ottoman Empire, already at an advanced stage of internal decay, represented the ideal diplomatic solution to Russia. As early as 1853, Tsar Nicholas I urged partition of the Ottoman Empire, suggesting that the European powers avoid war by ridding themselves of the Turkish "sick man" through gentlemanly means. But this idea remained anathema to Britain for another half century. Another approach found Russia participating, albeit often reluctantly, in multilateral negotiations, such as at the London Conference of 1871 and the Berlin Congress of 1878. These were convened to consider specific aspects of the Turkish question, particularly the regulations governing use of the Straits.

In 1798 and again in 1833, Russia, pursuing a third course, elected to support the Turks in the expectation that through alliance, rather than enmity, indirect influence at Constantinople or perhaps even outright concessions might be gained. A fourth alternative was simply to withdraw from the controversy and concentrate on domestic reforms. When this occurred it did so because the Russians accurately believed that the British were determined to keep the Turks in control of the Straits. But it only happened briefly—for example, during the rule of Alexander II—and it reflected a temporary acceptance of the limitations against expansion toward the Mediterranean Sea.

Though only two of the six basic policy options entailed actual hostilities, they figured so prominently as to dominate the entire period. Belligerence toward the Turks was a recurrent theme, prompting thirteen wars since 1677, the Crimean War being a classic example. Russian strategists at other times contemplated abandoning the Straits objective and pursuing instead the land route southward through the Caucasus, leading eventually to the warm-water ports of the Persian Gulf. This path, however, was blocked by the Kajar dynasty in Persia which defended the approaches to the Persian Gulf. Because Russia could never seriously expect to challenge Britain's position in India without access to the Gulf, the Russian tsars concentrated on conquering the Persian Empire, which would give them direct control over the gulf.[2] Cognizant of the strategic value of Persia, Britain strengthened its defensive capability for much the same reasons as it strengthened Turkey's. Despite British opposition, Russia persisted in involving itself in lengthy wars against the Persian Empire in 1804–13 and 1826–28. The Anglo-Russian agreement in 1907 to divide Persia into spheres of influence was the closest the tsars came to success on this front. Antecedents for the northern tier concept of Persia and Turkey serving as the forward defenses in a containment of Russia, with the dependable support of an outside third power, are found quite clearly in the nineteenth century.

No single policy, nor any combination of policies, enabled Russia to penetrate the Middle East by the beginning of the twentieth century. On the contrary, its position seemed weakened. The Sublime Porte lingered on in decentralized control of the Ottoman Empire. Its benefactor, Great Britain, actually had extended its sway over the entire region. Aden was occupied in 1839, and during the nineteenth century all the rulers and chieftains along the Persian Gulf coast—including Oman, the sheikhdoms of the Trucial Coast, Bahrein, and Kuwait —entered into close and "exclusive" treaty relations with the British government. Egypt was occupied in 1882; Cyprus was acquired through a Turkish concession in 1878; and a sphere of economic influence was established in Mesopotamia because of its proximity to India. Great Britain had grown to appreciate the strategic value of the Middle East as a result of two catalytic events, neither of British doing: Napoleon's invasion of Egypt in 1798 and the opening of the Suez Canal in 1869. Each event, resulting in new territorial acquisitions for the British Empire, contributed in turn to a more credible security system.

The Russo-Japanese War of 1904–5 offered indirect proof of Russia's impotence in the Mediterranean. In order to cope with the Japanese navy and to reinforce units in the Pacific, the Baltic squadron had to move from its home port 20,000 miles from the scene of hostilities, taking more than twice the time than if the route through the Mediterranean and the Suez Canal had been available. Exhausted by its ordeal, the Russian naval squadron was intercepted short of Vladivostok and annihilated in the Straits of Tsushima.

The lesson was not lost on Russia, as is evident from its territorial claims at the outset of the First World War. Once events found Russia allied with Britain against the Turks and Germany, the newest aspirant to hegemony through recourse to sea power, the Russian Foreign Ministry claimed annexation of Constantinople, both shores of the Bosphorus, the Sea of Marmara, and the Dardanelles as the minimum desiderata. The acceptance of these claims by England and France in March, 1915, represented a revolutionary transformation of western foreign policy vis-à-vis Russia. With Turkey prostrate by 1917, at last success was within Russia's reach. In view of the current Soviet appreciation for the Mediterranean, it is ironic that at that decisive moment Bolshevik renunciation of all earlier tsarist territorial claims should have kept Russia from at least sharing dual control of this sea with Britain more than fifty years ago.

During the interwar period, the Mediterranean and the Arab world did not figure prominently in Soviet foreign policy. The European countries, with their articulate proletarian classes, received greater attention from Lenin than did the backward societies of Asia, with their poor prospects for revolution. Nevertheless, the search for allies against capitalist encirclement led the Soviets to choose nationalist Turkey when it came time for them to enter into their first formal alliance with an outside power.

After the abortive Kronshtadt revolt by Russian

sailors against the Bolshevik regime in March, 1921, the navy was discredited and subordinated to the Red Army. In 1920 Trotsky had already summed up the navy's situation when he stated: "The Red Fleet has been weakened to the last degree—but it exists." This, too, diminished the possible importance of Middle Eastern waters for Soviet foreign policy. In any case, Britain offered every indication of remaining in effective control of the Mediterranean, the Persian Gulf, and all the lands between them. Turkish and Persian nationalism, drawing inspiration from past resistance against Russia, stiffened to preclude any possible Soviet encroachment, while the Arabs were hostile to the atheistic feature of communist ideology. In the 1930s, Arab nationalists were more interested in gaining independence than in restructuring the traditional Islamic society along Marxist lines.

These deterrents to successful Soviet penetration notwithstanding, the Middle East continued to be of more than passing interest to the new rulers of Russia. In secret negotiations with Nazi Germany during 1940 the Soviet Union made this interest explicit, declaring that its territorial aspirations centered "south of the national territory of the Soviet Union in the direction of the Indian Ocean."[3] A less known fact is that Stalin, in addition to staking out a political claim in the Middle East, also stressed the need for Russian naval mobility in any postwar settlement. During these same negotiations he gained German and Italian support for replacing the 1936 Montreux Convention governing the Turkish Straits; henceforth the Soviet Union was to have "the right of unrestricted passage of its navy through the Straits at any time." Germany's invasion of the Soviet Union once again frustrated the familiar political and military goals of Russian diplomacy; the United States and especially Great Britain were not prepared to make any such sweeping concessions.

After 1945, the Russians still had no capacity for ordering affairs in the Arab world and had little choice but to use indirect means to subvert the British position: endorsing partition (the favorite device of tsarist diplomacy) for Palestine; encouraging the defiance of the West by Iran's Tudeh Party and Prime Minister Mossadegh; and supporting local communist parties in Egypt, Syria, Iraq, and Jordan.[4] The United States, Britain, and France, by contrast, possessed as many as forty-three bases approachable from the Mediterranean. Nevertheless, the scales began to shift against the West in the aftermath of the Second World War. British resources were no longer sufficient to safeguard the empire; and Arab nationalism, growing in militancy, refused to fit itself neatly into western defense arrangements.

Circumstances by the mid-1950s had led to an affinity of interests and needs between Egypt and the Soviet Union. Egypt sought an alternative to dependence upon the West for aid and support, while the Kremlin needed some tangible proof of the efficacy of cultivating "progressive" regimes even under peaceful coexistence. President Nasser, by preventing the consolidation of the Baghdad Pact, thereby earned a debt of gratitude which the Kremlin acknowledged in the 1955 arms deal and has continued to pay through financing the Aswan Dam and equipping the Egyptian army.

In retrospect, the 1955 arms delivery to Egypt must be seen as a truly revolutionary development, for it enabled the Soviets finally to bypass the traditional northern tier barrier and to become actively involved in the intermediate southern tier from Egypt to Syria and Iraq. Despite this success at achieving a breakthrough, the opportunity had come too suddenly for the Soviets and not really at their initiative. They were as yet unprepared politically, militarily, and ideologically to grasp fully the implications inherent in a fluid and rapidly changing situation.

More recently Egypt has become the keystone for Russia's Middle Eastern policy, as it had been for Britain a century before. Over the years Soviet Russia increased its commitment to socialist Egypt and took whatever measures were deemed necessary—such as a naval presence off the Egyptian coast, or Soviet SAM–3 missiles and personnel introduced in 1970—to protect what was becoming a major foreign interest. An ideological justification for such an intimate relationship with Egypt was offered by *Pravda* in June, 1969, two years after that country's severe military setback. The Soviet commentator reasoned that

> . . . in the fifteen years of the existence of its anti-imperialist regime the U.A.R. has found political independence and national sovereignty. The omnipotence of the feudal lords and the big bourgeoisie connected with imperialism has ended. . . . Pursuing an independent, anti-imperialist foreign policy, the U.A.R. has won authority in the international arena and has established friendly ties and mutually profitable cooperation with the U.S.S.R. and the other socialist world countries. . . . The numerical strength of the working class is increasing and its authority and influence upon internal political life are growing.[5]

Operating from this strategic position, the Soviet Union proceeded to exploit unsettling conditions along the eastern Mediterranean and the Red Sea, which were caused by the concurrent rise of Arab nationalism and the decline of British imperialism. The main formula for success has been moderate progress. Overt aggression, for instance an invasion of Turkey or Iran, would have rallied the Middle Eastern countries into a regional defensive arrangement. Instead, indirect Soviet penetration represented a security problem for each individual country to handle separately. This approach left Britain, France, and the United States to pursue narrow self-interests. It also exploited the competitive nature of the region, setting Arab against Turk and Arab against Arab while encouraging continued strife between Arab and Israeli.

Thus, by 1960, the stage was set for a dramatic reversal of historical patterns. British policy was in the process of reorientating itself to "little England," the European continent, and the Common Market, and Russia was once again able to seek fulfillment on the oceans and toward the southern land mass of the Middle East, this time armed with an ideology which made expansion a moral imperative. Accelerating this process was the claim reasserted by the peoples of the region to be independent actors in determining their own political affiliation and, ultimately, their own destiny. Yet the region itself has not succeeded in escaping its customary role as a field of political struggle and intervention by outside powers.

Whatever future history may record of this new involvement by the Soviet Union in the Middle East, whatever imminent dilemmas lie in store for the Russian leadership, its status in the region at the start of the 1970s can only be regarded as a singular triumph from the perspective of the past.

IV. THE SOVIET INITIATIVE

Before 1967, and certainly before 1955, one could only speak of the Soviet Union *and* the Middle East in the sense of an aspiration; since then it is accurate to stress the reality of the Soviets *in* the Middle East. Russia's influence there has increased appreciably with the widening of its actual presence during the past decade. Such a trend is the product of a broad initiative using economics, diplomacy, and military arms for what are, in the last analysis, politico-strategic objectives. Having been unsuccessful in previous attempts, and perhaps already concerned with the dilemmas posed by success, the Soviets in their current venture are proceeding with somewhat more caution and with uncharacteristic patience and subtlety.

Evidence of Soviet influence is to be found in virtually every Arab country and at several social levels. The most telling sign in Moscow's favor is the increase in the number of revolutionary regimes in the area. Seizure of power in Libya, the Sudan, and Somalia by military officers eager for Soviet support occurred in rapid succession in the latter half of 1969. For the first time since its establishment in 1945, the Arab League came to be dominated by a majority of revolutionary states. It is now the traditional, western-oriented regimes who are on the defensive in intraregional politics.

The Soviet government has acted to strengthen these "progressive" military states, and in the process it has begun to derive benefits in concrete political and strategic terms as well as in prestige. The Soviet Union is their main supplier of modern weapons systems. It of-

38

fers training courses in Russian military academies, and its own military personnel and technicians serve as advisers to Middle Eastern armed forces, most notably in Egypt and Syria. Bilateral trade and cultural agreements have helped to extend the network of Soviet contacts from Rabat to Tehran.

Nor are its efforts necessarily restricted to the pro-Soviet regimes. Relations with Jordan have improved since 1967 when King Hussein visited Moscow, largely because of the latter's dissatisfaction with the stand taken by the American government after the Six-Day War. Soviet policy during the Lebanese crisis in 1969 in support of that country's sovereignty earned the praise of top Lebanese officials. Impressing both the revolutionary and conservative elements in the Arab world was the continuing visible presence of the Soviet navy in Middle Eastern waters.

The full extent and swiftness of Soviet penetration into the region during the 1960s can only be appreciated by comparing the position of the Soviet Union in 1970 with that of 1950. In that year Britain, France, and the United States could still reach agreement on regulating the sale of arms to the Middle East without serious concern for possible Soviet unilateral action.[1] The 1955 arms deal with Egypt signaled the end of this western monopoly on the supply of weapons; since then the Soviet bloc countries have become a principal supplier.[2] As a direct result, the elementary question of limiting arms exports to the volatile Middle East is complicated by conflicting aims and policies of the great powers. For example, France, acting ostensibly to exclude the Soviets as a supplier, has agreed to provide weapons to Libya, which Britain had contracted to supply originally. And the escalation in sophisticated weaponry, in both quality and quantity, continues unabated.

In U.N. deliberations on Palestine during 1947–48, one major concern of American policy makers had been to prevent Soviet exploitation of this dispute to gain a foothold anywhere in the Arab world. The U.S. endorsement of partition and, in April, 1948, of trusteeship was, at least in part, to prevent the formation of an international police force that might include a Soviet contingent.[3] Traces of this attitude were to be found as late as 1956 when the United Nations Emergency Force came into being, composed solely of units from the smaller powers. By 1969, however, it was certainly apparent that the Soviets, by their naval presence and advisory capacity in Arab military affairs, had long since ended western regional exclusiveness. Indeed, in western capitals there was growing concern that Soviet ascendancy might lead eventually to a Kremlin policy of sole proprietorship.

The effort to establish a Middle East agreement through pressure from the great powers provides a third example of the Soviet involvement in that region. Whether discussions were conducted on the two-power or the four-power level, in either case the Soviet Union was recognized as a participant; its influence and consent would be necessary if a solution were to have any chance of success. Such a notion would have been unthinkable ten years ago.

The diversity, scope, and intensity of the Soviet effort give clear evidence that Russia has ended the ambivalence toward the southern tier that had characterized its earlier policy. The Russians have also adopted different tactics toward their traditional opponents, Turkey and Iran. The incentive for the Soviet initiative is provided by the international equilibrium, or the "strategic stabilization" of the Cold War. The opportunity for it is provided by the dislocating effects of transition in the

Middle East. The pattern of British control, in its broad outlines, suggests an adaptable model full of insights and precedents. Geography and history, lastly, serve as both a challenge and a source of inspiration for the Russian leadership.

The new approach toward the Middle East in the 1960s is a product of Soviet attitudes toward the contemporary international scene in general. This developed in five distinct phases. The first necessitated no less than a fundamental reappraisal of Cold War tenets which had been regarded as sacrosanct during the 1950s. During much of this period the Dulles-Radford doctrine of massive retaliation, as a reaction to the Korean experience of renewed communist aggression, governed East-West strategic thought and planning. Within the military circles of both blocs it gave way slowly to the alternative doctrines of limited war and flexible response. Numerous situations could be conceived in which thermonuclear war, if not unthinkable, would certainly not be imperative.[4] In instances of limited war a premium had to be placed on a wide selection of responses, including such elements of the traditional military arsenal as naval power and such unorthodox forms of conquest as subversion, insurgency, and guerrilla warfare. Washington and Moscow, endowed with a nuclear capability, simultaneously recognized the importance of being able to wage limited war, and each sought to cultivate what Henry Kissinger has termed "a feeling for nuance." The only other alternatives consisted of a choice between total war or the equally unacceptable alternatives of ineffective resistance or capitulation.

From the standpoint of Soviet policy, global strategy needed to be revised. It had to be capable of preventing by limited means western success in areas of Soviet interest, but at the same time it had to prove itself adaptable to the spirit of unceasing communist pressure embodied in the principle of peaceful coexistence.[5] From this same perspective, the countries of the Third World were open to indirect involvement and political gain not requiring a commitment of maximum force. In the early 1960s, the Kremlin was still preoccupied with the question of conducting general nuclear war; nevertheless, increased recognition was accorded as well to prospects of local wars and to facilitating so-called "wars of national liberation"—to be conducted by proxy without allowing them to escalate uncontrollably, and irretrievably, into global nuclear conflict.[6]

Political-strategic thinking along the lines of limited war and a flexible response to challenges and opportunities alike demanded an ability to project various forms of national power great distances and at great speed. The second component affecting Soviet attitudes toward the Middle East is, therefore, tactical. It is evidenced today by the development of a strong naval capability as part of the build-up in strategic delivery forces.[7] As early as 1956, Marshal Zhukov, then Soviet defense minister, shed light on this new element of Soviet contingency planning. Military experts, he explained, held that naval warfare would acquire greater significance in a future war if the Soviets could build a strong navy.[8] The open seas are appreciated as a medium by which to project or to enhance one's power, even in the nuclear space age. That the Soviet Union and its European satellites have had to face a global coalition of maritime powers is yet another incentive to seek a minimum of naval parity.

Already under Khrushchev, but more noticeably under his successors, an upgrading of the navy took place. Considerable expenditure was incurred in constructing a modern ocean-going navy, marked by the building of the first two Soviet helicopter carriers, the *Moskva* and the *Leningrad*. Nuclear missile-bearing submarines have received particular attention in enhancing Soviet flexibility. Russia possesses the fastest growing merchant marine; its fishing fleet, deploying four thousand craft, is the world's largest, and is often used for intelligence purposes.[9]

Concomitant areas of Soviet naval capacity are being thoroughly revived. The question of amphibious landing capabilities is increasingly being analyzed in Soviet military literature. Since 1964, the marines have had a special status and table of organization. Similarly, the missile-launching submarines are evaluated highly, while the vulnerability of aircraft carriers is also recognized. Procedures involved in refueling and repairs while at sea are being improved as well.

Soviet naval ascendance has been accompanied, at a third level, by a greater respect for the geostrategic centrality of the Middle East. Defensively, it guards the southern frontier of the Soviet Union and affords protection in depth for the Russian heartland. Offensively, because of its strategic waterways, the region is a key to Asia and Africa; and, in the struggle between capitalism and communism, "the fate of Russian progress depends upon whom seventy underdeveloped countries choose to follow."[10] Its suitability as a target for renewed effort was all the more enhanced by the demise of British power and influence and the difficulties being encountered by the United States in retaining its weak grip over the region.

Fresh priorities in the Middle East, in turn, stimulated a review of the past historical relationship. Penetration, it was concluded, might better be achieved by subtle measures—by exploiting insecurities and deficiencies within the region—than by the blunt force so characteristic of the traditional Russian approach to its southern neighbors. Current Soviet policy shows a willingness to accept gradual gains instead of expecting an immediate advantage or a sudden shift in the balance of power. Interest in this particular region means working with, rather than suppressing, the peoples of the Middle East, or, alternatively, of ignoring the region entirely until conditions might be ripe for proletarian revolutions in the orthodox interpretation of communist doctrine.

A fifth adjustment has therefore been necessary, and in the most sensitive area of ideology, which is also the least conducive to change. Kremlin theoreticians nonetheless provided the requisite sanction during the 1960s by relegating the class struggle to a position of secondary importance. They are stressing instead an anti-imperialist bond with the recently emergent nations. This alteration, most useful for operating in the Arab world and in other areas of the Third World, has been articulated on numerous occasions. One Soviet commentator stated in 1966, "It would be the worst example of blind dogmatism and the greatest strategic error in the struggle for the socialist transformation of the world to reject the revolutionary democrats because their views are at variance with Marxism."[11] At the height of the Middle East crisis in 1967, Prime Minister Kosygin provided official confirmation of this trend in Soviet policy during his appearance before the General Assembly of the United Nations. Espousing the cause of national liberation, he indicated a Russian responsibility for "rendering aid to the victim of aggression and supporting the peoples who fight for their independence and freedom."[12] Since then the Soviet Union has consistently sought to identify itself with those "progressive" regimes in the Middle East and northern Africa.

Any such rendering of tangible aid and support naturally implies the ability to deliver it expeditiously to the recipient. That this capability and the theoretical reorientations were nonexistent before 1960 is apparent from the failure of the Soviets to fully capitalize on opportunities in the Middle East which attended the weakening of British control. The futility of cultivating overseas interests without a commensurate naval strength was confirmed dramatically for the Russians by the Cuban missile crisis in 1962. It proved conclusively that deploying and sustaining instruments of policy beyond one's shores require an all-important tactical and logistical underpinning.

The Cuban experience, therefore, acted as the catalyst for a program already underway in the Soviet Union to construct a modern, efficient, multipurpose navy. In the process the navy has been transformed from a mere adjunct to static forces into a fleet capable of supporting Soviet interests in more remote parts of the globe.

The Soviet squadron in the Mediterranean, part of the Black Sea Fleet, made its appearance in 1964 and numbered about 25 vessels.[13] Because world attention was focused on the Arab-Israeli crisis in 1967, the substantial increase in the Soviet presence escaped general notice: the Turkish Foreign Ministry reported that 157 vessels passed from the Black Sea to the Mediterranean that year.[14] Since then, the Soviet naval presence has fluctuated from 30 ships to 60 or more. While still inferior to the 2 or 3 carriers and 200 aircraft of the Sixth Fleet, this force now includes warships armed with a variety of missiles, amphibious ships with naval infantry, a helicopter carrier, nuclear submarines, and auxiliary vessels.[15]

The strenuous effort to achieve prominence as a global sea power bore fruit in two recent episodes. In March,

1969, western observers were discomfited by the movement of twenty major Soviet warships from the Norwegian Sea to the North Atlantic—the largest Soviet naval force to do so since the Second World War. Speculation immediately arose in the European press over their ultimate destination and mission: to challenge NATO ships in the Atlantic; to strengthen the Soviet naval presence in the Mediterranean during renewed fighting between Israel and Egypt; or to assume positions in the Far East at the time of Sino-Soviet clashes on the Ussuri River.[16]

That the squadron merely engaged in conventional sea exercises before returning to port need not detract from its dual significance, for it aroused serious western concern over the broader range of political and military options now opening to the Soviet Union through sea power. It confirmed earlier Russian boasts to the effect that "the time when Russia could be kept out of the world's oceans has gone forever. We will sail all the world's seas. No force on earth can prevent us." Confirmation was given in July of that year when a Soviet flotilla appeared off the eastern coast of the United States, sailed in the Caribbean, and paid an official visit to Cuba. Nothing better could contrast with the Soviet impotence in 1962.

These two episodes demonstrated the power, range, and options of the Soviet navy. But the navy's presence in the North Atlantic and Caribbean was transitory, whereas in the Mediterranean it has all the aspects of being permanent. The growing frequency of visits by Soviet warships in both the Red Sea and Persian Gulf further establishes the Soviets as an interested party in the waters connecting the Middle East with Asia and Africa.

Soviet propaganda, in strengthening this image, has

consistently emphasized two points. First, the Soviet presence is justified in terms of its concern with what transpires beyond its southern frontier, and in terms of its leadership of the world revolutionary movements. An early attempt at legitimatizing Soviet interest in Middle Eastern affairs was made in May, 1967, just prior to the outbreak of hostilities. The Soviet government keeps a close watch on developments in the Near East, the official news agency TASS maintained, because "the maintenance of peace and security in the area directly adjacent to the Soviet borders meets the *vital interests* of the Soviet peoples."[17]

Second, Soviet spokesmen seek to discredit the U.S. Sixth Fleet, describing its personnel as "gendarmes of international reaction," and to deny its right to be in the region. They wonder how the Americans can argue that the presence of the fleet "is perfectly natural," when "the U.S.A. is thousands of kilometers away and has no direct connection" with the Arab world.[18] One Soviet analyst, purporting to speak on behalf of the "tens of millions of people who live in southern Europe, North Africa and the Near East," insisted that the Sixth Fleet "must get out beyond Gibraltar, back to American harbors."[19]

The navy in Middle Eastern waters is now a major instrument of Soviet foreign policy in the region and beyond. In this, as in a striking number of other aspects, the Soviets are following the general strategy that the British had used to dominate the region.

With regard to the northern tier countries of Turkey and Iran, the Soviet Union has come to realize that outright control of these countries is unnecessary to the pursuit of national and imperial interests. Security along the southern frontier of Russia may be achieved through a policy of good neighborliness aimed at neutralizing the two countries rather than at compromising their political sovereignty. Like the British before them, the Soviets are seeking through amicable relations to ensure access to the Mediterranean and the Persian Gulf and to foster economic ties.

The foundation for a rapprochement between Moscow and Ankara, from the Turkish standpoint, has been provided by the changing nature of Cold War doctrines. American hesitancy in guaranteeing full support for its NATO allies occasioned serious concern in the Turkish capital in the early 1960s. Until then the Turks had considered that as members of NATO they were covered by the U.S. nuclear umbrella, interpreting the treaty literally that an attack on one member was tantamount to an attack on all. They began to sense that the United States, reluctant to incur any Soviet nuclear retaliation, was hesitant to share this interpretation. If this was the case, the United States might very well back off from a confrontation with the Soviet Union in a cloud of rhetoric rather than neutrons. Washington did not hasten to dispel such fears. Particularly vulnerable because of its forward geographical position, and sensitive about its national independence after centuries of defending it from Russian encroachment, Turkey did not want to be exposed once again to Soviet incursions or political pressure. Hence it was in the Turkish interest, too, to improve relations with the northern neighbor; this acceptance coincided with the willingness of the Soviets to deal with Turkey on the basis of national equality and respect.

The immobilization of NATO, hastened by a decline in French enthusiasm under President de Gaulle, provided a second incentive for Turkey. It made even less credible the security guarantee which the Turks needed from the West in order to defy the Soviet Union.

Similarly, when the conception of world politics as a state of rigid bipolarity lost validity, the Turks began to sense the advantages accruing from neutralism. However, the primary incentive for an independent Turkish policy stemmed from dissatisfaction with the stand taken by the United States over the issue of Cyprus. Ankara was disappointed when the United States refused to permit an invasion of Cyprus at the end of 1963; this facilitated Russian attempts for better relations with Turkey, which had begun after the fall of Menderes in 1960.

Prime Minister Demirel, upon ending a visit to Russia in September, 1967, noted that "the last traces of hostility" with the Soviet Union had been eliminated. As a result of improved relations with Turkey, the Soviet Union derives three important benefits. There is no longer a serious possibility of a western attack on Russia from Turkish territory. The large number of intermediate-range missiles previously positioned inside Turkey were removed after 1963 in favor of Polaris submarines stationed at sea. Second, the present Russo-Turkish détente affords a greater degree of bilateral trade. In 1969, there were about one-thousand Soviet technicians in Turkey to supervise construction of six industrial plants being financed on liberal terms by Moscow. Trade between the two countries has expanded from $15 million in 1964 to an estimated $81 million in 1969. Turkish President Cevdet Sunay paid a goodwill visit to the Soviet Union in November, 1969, as a further sign of mutual efforts to continue the peaceful coexistence between the two historical rivals. Should Soviet relations ever proceed to such a point where Turkey might consider severing its ties with NATO, the loss of nearly sixteen Turkish divisions would deal a sharp blow to Western Europe's perimeter defense.

A third asset, and the one most important for Russia's future relationship with the Third World, is the ability to pass through the Dardanelles without opposition from Turkey. Although rejecting Soviet efforts at revising the 1936 Montreux Convention, the Ankara government permits unrestricted passage to Russian warships. Conversely, leftist and student agitation within Turkey has made that country less hospitable to visits by the U.S. Sixth Fleet.

The Turkish government is able to use its policy toward the Arabs as a bargaining point with Moscow, too. Pro-Arab statements and endorsements of the demand made by Russia and the Arabs that Israel withdraw from captured Arab territories were bound to impress the Kremlin leaders. A far more difficult problem for Turkey has been Soviet efforts to use Turkey as an air corridor for transferring arms and planes to the Arab countries. Forced into this awkward position, testing its goodwill toward the Soviet Union while a member of NATO, Ankara has forbidden overflights by planes carrying communist weapons to the Arabs; however, to the displeasure of its western allies, it has continued to allow Soviet-built jets to land and refuel in Turkey en route to Arab air forces.

Mutual self-interest also appears to have dominated relations between the Soviet Union and Iran. During the 1960s the Shah of Iran proved adroit in maintaining correct if not cordial relations with the Soviet Union. Here again the realities of geography and Cold War diplomacy imposed themselves. Too close an identification with the West was likely to arouse Soviet concern and animosity; at the same time, being taken for granted as a confirmed ally of the West could reduce Iran's bargaining position with the United States. In 1962 the Shah assured Moscow that no foreign rocket bases would be permitted on Iranian soil; in the following year First Secretary of the Communist Party Leonid Brezhnev was officially received in Tehran. The Shah himself paid a state visit to Russia in June, 1965, after which a joint communiqué was issued noting satisfaction on both sides that Soviet-Iranian relations were developing "auspiciously."

In pursuing a policy of reconciliation and cooperation with Iran, the Russians and East Europeans have been stressing economic relations as a means of acquiring political influence; the British had done likewise. In 1965, Iran ceased to receive military and economic aid from the United States, being regarded by the latter as having reached the stage of economic takeoff. Seizing the initiative, the Soviets negotiated an agreement in January, 1966, with Iran. According to the terms of the contract, Iran has promised to supply the Russians with up to 10 billion cubic meters of natural gas per year between 1970 and 1985. The gas, estimated to be worth $600 million, will be transported via a pipeline from oil fields on the Persian Gulf to the Caspian frontier.[20] The Soviet Union, in return, is assisting in laying the pipeline and is constructing a steel mill. An additional incentive for Iran is the opportunity to transport goods through Soviet territory, including use of the Volga-Balt waterway, which is the shortest route to a number of Eastern European ports and which makes Iran independent of the Suez Canal.

A 1967 Soviet-Iranian trade agreement calls for $540 million in bilateral trade over a five-year period. Of particular significance is the agreement by the Soviets to supply some $110 million worth of military equipment to the Iranian army. In April, 1968, Kosygin paid a visit to Iran which resulted in a Soviet offer of up to $300 million in credits for the purchase of Soviet capital and industrial goods. The Czechs have agreed to buy $200 million worth of oil from Iran between 1970 and 1980. Aside from oil, an estimated 27 percent of Iranian exports now go to Eastern European countries. Both Turkey and Iran have a substantial interest in jointly constructing a pipeline linking Iran's Khuzestan oil-fields to the Turkish Mediterranean port of Iskanderun, thus profiting from the supply and shipment of oil and natural gas to energy-deficient Eastern Europe.

Soviet accomplishments in Turkey and Iran are directly related to the present struggle over the Middle East. In the first instance, they have provided Russia with a greater sense of security along its southern frontier. This, in turn, enables the Soviet leadership to devote greater attention to the Arab world lying exposed just beyond the northern tier. It is a luxury not enjoyed by the Russians in decades or centuries past. A principal manifestation is certainly Soviet egress from the Turkish Straits and visits by warships of the Red Navy to the Iranian port of Bandar Abbas, on the Strait of Hormuz, which controls the entrance to the Persian Gulf. Calculations of self-interest thus have led both Turkey and Iran to improved relations with their colossus of the north. These have already facilitated the renewed attempt at establishing a more durable presence in the Arab world; to the extent that they are built on a firm foundation, these relations will figure even more prominently in Middle Eastern affairs in the future.

In the southern tier, the Soviets have singled out several countries for particular attention. Of central importance for an understanding of the Soviet initiative is its relationship with Egypt. Following the British precedent, the Russians view Egypt as the keystone to ascendancy in the adjacent lands and seas. They are mindful perhaps of Leibnitz's dictum in the seventeenth century: "The possession of Egypt opens the way to conquests worthy of Alexander. Whoever has Egypt will have all the coasts and islands of the Indian Ocean."

The Aswan Dam, a refurbished Egyptian army, Soviet technicians and military advisers, aid and industrial projects, diplomatic support, praise of Egyptian efforts at socialist progress in the Soviet press, and the presence of naval vessels along the Egyptian coast to deter possible Israeli attack—these, individually and collectively, dramatize the very heavy commitment being made by the Soviet Union to Egypt's destiny. The radar and missile installations placed in early 1970 around Alexandria, Cairo's airport, and the Aswan Dam have added to the commitment. The visit to Moscow in November, 1969, by a high-ranking Egyptian delegation, headed by Anwar al-Sadat, Foreign Minister Mahmoud Riad, and Minister of War General Muhammad Fawzi, is but one example of the close consultation and collaboration between Cairo and Moscow on diplomatic, political, and military policy.

Soviet support, tangible and inspirational, is partially responsible for three primary elements of Egyptian foreign policy: hostility toward the United States and the West; leadership in inter-Arab affairs; and a hard line toward Israel—consisting of a refusal to enter into negotiations aimed at a comprehensive peace settlement and a willingness to enter into a "fourth round" of hostilities, likely to implicate the superpowers as well. The Egyptians have taken pains to acknowledge their debt to the Soviet Union publicly.[21] Egypt has also compensated Russia by giving Soviet ships easy access to Alexandria and Port Said.

If and when the Suez Canal is reopened, its availability to the Red Navy will be guaranteed by the strong

Soviet presence in Egypt. There is little doubt but that the canal's value to the West has diminished as a result of its protracted closures in 1956 and since 1967. Western oil and shipping interests, having learned from their costly experiences, are ordering supertankers too large for passage through the canal. They are also becoming accustomed to the longer route around the Cape of Good Hope. From the Soviet view, however, the canal would still represent a vital strategic point enabling Russian ships to move swiftly toward objectives in the Indian Ocean and the Far East. Trade with the Third World, which has more than doubled between 1958 and 1967, would be facilitated, too. Should Soviet regional influence embolden its leaders to attempt at some future point a radical shift in the global balance of power by such offensive actions as denial of Middle Eastern oil to the West or interference with international maritime commerce, control of the Suez Canal would be a key factor.

Soviet efforts in the Arab world also have been aimed at a strengthening of influence in both Syria and Iraq. Relations with Syria began in the 1950s when, aside from Egypt, the Soviet Union found little receptivity elsewhere in the region to its offers of friendship. At times the extremism of the Syrian revolutionary military leaders has become a source of annoyance to the Kremlin. In defending Lebanon during its internal crisis in 1969, the Soviets could not have been too pleased when Damascus contributed to the tension by moving troops to the border of Lebanon and by supporting its infiltration by Syrian-organized paramilitary groups. One compensation for the Soviets, however, is the use of Latakia as a major naval port in the eastern Mediterranean.

Iraq holds a comparable position for Soviet strategic policy in the Persian Gulf. Just as the British valued

Iraq highly, so too the Soviets, who have developed an appreciation for the rich oil deposits located in the Persian Gulf. A broad agreement was reached with the Iraqi government in December, 1968, to permit Russian technicians to carry out oil exploration in the North Rumaila section of the country. Predictions that the Soviet Union will become a net importer of oil in this decade and will no longer be able to supply its European satellites, help to explain the recent communist interest in the politics and economics of oil in the Persian Gulf.[22] Iraq and Iran, having both oil and proximity to Russia, could become its major suppliers of oil, especially if overland communication routes are improved by new roads and pipelines.

The imminent departure of the British from the Persian Gulf also enhances the value of Iraq for Soviet policy. Revolutionary Iraq shares in the Soviet desire to prevent the United States from filling the vacuum left by Great Britain. The two countries have a common interest in frustrating western efforts at creating a federation of the seven Trucial sheikhdoms with Bahrein and Qatar. An earlier attempt at union failed in 1967 in Southern Yemen and resulted in a leftist, pro-Soviet regime. The Iraqi port of Umm Qasr has also been opened to Soviet warships. The first naval visit to the Persian Gulf took place in May, 1968, just four months after Prime Minister Wilson informed the House of Commons and the world of Britain's intention to effect a pullout east of Suez.

Southern Yemen is yet another focal point for the Soviets. In present evaluations of the region, it should not be forgotten that the imperial outpost at Aden occupied a primary place in British strategic policy. The British, during the second half of the nineteenth century, showed how control of Aden and the nearby

Straits of Bab al-Mandab might be used for dominating the Arabian peninsula, the Persian Gulf and its sheikhdoms, East Africa, the southern exit from the Red Sea, and the Indian Ocean. In February, 1969, the Soviet government offered Southern Yemen economic and cultural aid as well as military assistance. A coup which was carried out in September, 1969, brought to power a more leftist regime under Abdul Fattah Ismail dedicated to strengthening ties with the Soviet Union and to implementing Marxism internally.

The Soviet initiative extends as well to the western littoral of the Red Sea. Seizure of power by military forces in Somalia in October, 1969, and their declaration of a Somali Democratic Republic has opened a new potential outlet for Soviet influence in East Africa. The supply of military equipment and the strong irridentist component in Somali nationalism is likely to increase tension along the Horn of Africa. Somalia in the past has laid claims to territory now held by Ethiopia and Kenya. A renewal of such claims would further weaken these prowestern states. Both suffer already from two serious internal problems: succession and secession. The political future and foreign policy orientation of both countries are made uncertain by the question of who will succeed Emperor Haile Selassie and President Jomo Kenyatta. In addition, Ethiopia has had to cope with a violent nationalist movement in Eritrea which, if successful, would deprive Addis Ababa of Assab and Massawa, its sole outlets to the Red Sea. Kenya's future is jeopardized by the fissiparous tendencies of tribalism which surfaced once again following the assassination of Tom Mboya.

One possible indicator of the growing interest of the Soviet Union in East and North Africa is reflected in the flights made by Aerofloat, the state-owned Soviet airline. As of October, 1969, it was second only to Pan-American, serving twelve countries in Africa. These countries were: Uganda, Tanzania, Somalia, Morocco, Tunisia, Sudan, Guinea, Senegal, Egypt, Mali, Algeria, and Kenya; in addition, Yemen and Southern Yemen were other stops en route to Africa. The Soviet airline is likely to assume greater importance as a means of extending contact and influence. As it does so, the Middle East, an air corridor between Russia and Africa, will also figure more prominently in Soviet economic and commercial strategy.

Political developments in Sudan within the last year have led to an increase in the Soviet presence in that country, too. The revolutionary government, since its coup in September, 1969, has shown greater militancy on the Arab-Israeli question and has sought closer relations with Moscow. Two months after the coup, the chairman of the Sudanese Revolutionary Council, General Ja'afar Muhammad al-Numairy, was received warmly in the Kremlin. As a result of his visit, a protocol on the extension of trade relations was signed; agreement was reached on a program of cultural and scientific cooperation; and Soviet Premier Alexei Kosygin, President Nikolai Podgorny, and First Secretary Leonid Brezhnev accepted an invitation to visit Sudan.

In North Africa, the Soviets, this time borrowing from the French model, regard Algeria as the most worthy of support. Taking up much of the slack left by the termination of French colonialism, they have furnished credits and substantial amounts of military equipment to the revolutionary government. This pattern, reinforced by periodic visits of high-ranking Soviet military, cultural, and political delegations, extends as well to neighboring Morocco. The fact that Morocco is usually regarded as being prowestern and is ruled by a conservative monarchy has not precluded Soviet interest and moderate investment. One result is to extend Soviet influence along the eastern Mediterranean, bringing it close to Gibraltar.

The revolution that took place in Libya in September, 1969, must be regarded at present as a major windfall for the Soviet Arab policy. In the immediate sense, it established yet another socialist military regime in the Arab world favorably inclined toward the Soviet Union. Together with Sudan, it indirectly strengthened the Soviets by enhancing the prestige of President Nasser on Egypt's western and southern frontiers and by broadening the anti-Israel and antiwestern coalition of Arab states.

In the long-term, Libya's loss to the West may well prove to have tipped the scales decisively in favor of the Soviets. The problem of succession was acute and obvious in Libya; King Idris was over eighty years of age and in failing health, while the Crown Prince had shown himself to be lacking in the qualities of leadership. Western military and commercial interests were long-standing and substantial. Libyan security forces had been trained and equipped by the United States and Great Britain since independence in 1952. Yet the two western powers failed to so influence events or to win the support of the young Libyan military officers in order to safeguard their interests and retain the country within the western camp. Nor can the usual explanation of American weakness in the Middle East because of close identification with Israel explain this significant setback, for Libya had been a disinterested party to the Arab-Israeli dispute throughout.

What became increasingly clear at the close of 1969, however, was that western interests in Libya were jeopardized. Restrictions were placed on foreign personnel; the United States was attacked in the local press; Libyan troops were reportedly sent to Suez and Jordan against Israel; western banks were nationalized; and cancellation of a £100 million order for an air defense system from Britain threatened to strike another blow at the stability of the pound sterling and at the British balance of payments.

Even worse, from the strategic point of view, was the insistence of the revolutionary government that the United States evacuate Wheelus Air Force Base, built at a cost of approximately $100 million, before the contract expired in 1970; the British agreed to do likewise from their air base at el-Adem, near Tobruk. From these air bases, now being condemned as symbols of "western imperialism," the United States and Britain were able in the past to provide air cover over the entire eastern Mediterranean and thereby to strengthen the credibility of the Sixth Fleet.

The recent entry of Libya as a major exporter of oil made the country even more of a long-range strategic asset to the West. More than three million barrels of oil are pumped daily from Libyan fields. In 1968, revenue from exports amounted to $1 billion, 99 percent of which derived from oil sales; Libya has already become second to Iran as the largest oil-producing nation in the Middle East and North Africa, surpassing Saudi Arabia.[23] The uniqueness of Libya, and its value to Western Europe, lies in its independence of the Suez Canal and its proximity to the industrial centers of Europe. The region's other major oil exporters—Saudi Arabia, Iran, Iraq, and the Persian Gulf producers—as well as European buyers are dependent upon oil tankers sailing either through the canal or around Africa, or else upon pipelines running through Jordan, Israel, Syria, and Lebanon. They are thus subject to higher shipping costs and to interference by outside forces, whereas Libya could provide fast, dependable service even in times of crisis and tension in other parts of the Arab world. The West can no longer count on such an advantage.

The Soviet Union, on the other hand, may show itself eager to utilize these economic and strategic advantages. Libya's oil output might be diverted to Eastern European markets, and its air bases could be opened to the Soviet air force. Those analysts who disparage the military significance of the Soviet naval presence in the Mediterranean have pointed to the lack of air cover for the Russian vessels. Flights from Wheelus, however, in conjunction with bases in Algeria and Egypt, would erase this strategic deficiency. The Russians, in any case, are well on their way to achieving that goal of political influence in Libya which had been so effectively denied them by the western powers since 1945.

The British, in securing their primacy over the Middle East and in guarding the main avenues of transit to India, established direct control over several posts and bases ringing the area. From these points on the periphery of the Arab world, they advanced inland and gradually involved themselves in regional politics. Similarly, economic interests were developed which they tended to regard as vital. In this sense, too, the symmetry between British imperialism and the current Soviet initiative is holding true. There is one major distinction, however, which is the result of a difference in technique between nineteenth- and late twentieth-century statecraft: The Soviets, have not assumed direct control over any country or military base. As a concession to the sensitivities of Third World nationalism, and out of political expediency, the Kremlin has contented itself with preponderant influence and indirect control over the most important strategic points. It derives satisfaction merely from the use of port facilities, anchorage rights, and warehouses for stockpiling parts and equipment. These moderate requests are usually granted willingly by the local authorities, who have welcomed this new source of revenue since the closure of the Suez Canal and the departure of their former French and British customers.

Whether as a primary objective or merely as a derivative of their broad initiative, the Soviets have acquired access rights to many of the excellent ports in the region so highly valued by Great Britain and France. These include: Latakia, Alexandria, Port Said, Hodeida, Basra, Umm Qasr, Aden, Berbera, and Khorramshahr. Barring any crisis in Soviet-Algerian relations, Moscow can be expected to utilize the facilities of Mers el-Kebir vacated by the French. Moving freely from the Black Sea into the Mediterranean, the Soviet navy is able to avail itself of port facilities in the eastern Mediterranean and North Africa, all along the Red Sea and northward through the Persian Gulf. The way is being paved therefore for a further thrust eastward, leading to the creation of a Soviet presence "east of Suez" and in the Indian Ocean.

This concern with the seas and ports of the Middle East has resulted in a Soviet innovation in relations with the Arab countries—maritime aid. In 1958 the Soviets undertook construction of the Hodeida port for Yemen, which was then still a reactionary monarchy. Work began in 1962 on a deep-water port at Berbera. The Russians are busy building shipyards at Basra and Alexandria, improving Aden's harbors and docks, providing Algeria with oil tankers, aiding Iraq in studying and surveying the Tigris River between Baghdad and Mosul, and helping Southern Yemen with its fishing industry, canning factories, and navigation. Such forms of maritime aid clearly enable the Soviets to place naval experts in these several countries while providing a cover for gathering intelligence under the guise of economic assistance.

Maritime aid is but one element of the Soviet policy of indirect penetration. Other traditional means of gaining influence in the Middle East are being used to advantage also. Friendships are cultivated by economic trade and aid, weapons supplies, cultural exchanges, and diplomatic visits. The Soviet presence is then reinforced by advisers, technicians, military instructors, and permanent diplomatic missions. Finally, periodic visits by the Red Navy—"showing of the flag"—offer a tangible demonstration of Soviet power which cannot but impress itself psychologically on the beholder. As an instrument of marked economy of force, the navy enables the Kremlin to exert its influence on the land and governments of the Middle East as well.

As a result of all this expenditure, assiduous cultivation of friendly ties, and the exploitation of events and dynamic forces, the Soviet Union finds itself in an ascendant position in the Middle East. It provides a wide range of options in the region and beyond, but not without posing certain dilemmas for the Kremlin. At the same time it carries serious implications both for the regional members and for the West, particularly the United States.

Some observers may choose to evaluate the Soviet initiative, and its success thus far, as the preface to an era of Russian mastery in the lands between the eastern Mediterranean and the Indian Ocean. Others, more appreciative of the intricacies and inconsistencies still to be found in that region, tend to discount the likelihood of Soviet permanence. Rather, they cite the strength of Arab nationalism and the unpredictability of the Arabs as sufficient cause to view the Soviet Union as a temporary element in the Middle East. The outcome will depend ultimately on two sets of variables: (1) how the Soviets and Arabs relate to each other in the future and (2) what form of response will be forthcoming from the rival superpower, the regional states, and the regional organizations from Europe to Asia, both individually and collectively.

V. THE SOVIET-ARAB RELATIONSHIP: AN UNCERTAIN PROSPECTUS

During the 1960s the Soviet Union marked the Middle East as both worthy of and open to a serious political initiative. The Turkish, Persian, and Arab inhabitants of the region have facilitated this campaign by their undisguised receptivity. In terms of the 1970s, however, where are these tangible political and strategic gains likely to lead the Soviets? What do they seek in the Middle East? And toward what policy ends can their newly acquired prominence in this region be employed in terms of the larger international contest of power?

It is important to keep in mind that in many ways Soviet entry into the Arab Middle East has been less the function of conscious design than of opportunism, though both factors were at work. Regional instability and the British withdrawal provided an opportunity which the Soviets recognized only belatedly. After the Second World War they exploited every situation to hasten the loss of Britain's hold over the region, but they were unable to capitalize on these situations for their own direct gain. In the 1950s, though the Soviets recognized the innovations in the Arab world, they were unable to make these changes of practical significance. More recently the Soviets have made the four requisite adjustments—in global strategy, tactics, diplomacy, and ideology—which have enabled them to effect a comprehensive penetration of the region. There is little evidence, however, to suppose that the Soviet leadership has laid down a specific set of limitations and objectives for itself in the Middle East.

Improved relations with Turkey and Iran, after all, would seem to satisfy the minimal desideratum of security in an area contiguous to the Soviet homeland. The containment policy of the West is undermined; the northern tier countries are largely neutralized; and a long period of Soviet economic, political, and military exclusion is terminated. What need, therefore, of the Arabs?

Even if the need is accepted as a reasonable outcome and extension of the Soviet sphere of influence southward, why has the Kremlin been so indiscriminate in its quest for clients and friends in the Arab world? The position already acquired in Egypt and Syria after 1955 seemingly should have sufficed to end the western monopoly in the southern tier of the Middle East and in the eastern Mediterranean while at the same time substantiating the Soviet Union's claim as a power of truly global dimensions. Nor from a regional context were Syria and Egypt merely marginal political units: Damascus and Cairo had been two principal centers for Arab nationalism and for attempts at social and economic modernization since the nineteenth century. By any standard of measure Syria and Egypt would be guaranteed a voice in future regional politics, and through them the Soviet Union.

Nevertheless, the U.S.S.R. did not content itself with these impressive gains. It showed itself amenable to the entreaties of almost any Arab petitioner. Moscow became the protector of the revolutionary states. At the same time, it was not above dealing with conservative or even reactionary states, having agreed already in 1957 to sell arms to the feudal monarchy then in power in Yemen. Moscow recognized Kuwait in 1963 and Jordan in 1964. Nor have the Russians avoided identifying themselves with the various national liberation movements throughout the region; communist arms are being used by insurgent groups in Muscat and Oman, in Bahrein and Kuwait, and along the Horn of Africa. Each of these contacts represents, in varying degree, a form of Soviet undertaking and commitment.

This aspect of unselectivity in the Soviet approach to the Middle East can be attributed to several compelling factors. One is the dynamic nature of power politics, whereby a state is encouraged to go beyond parity and to pursue a comparative, or even absolute, advantage over its rivals. Moreover, advocates of moderation are at a distinct disadvantage whenever their country's policy continues to meet with success—what Halford Mackinder referred to as "the momentum of the Going Concern." In the case of the Soviet adventure in the Middle East, having seen they could penetrate without increasing risk of counterpressure, much less of war, they gradually increased their commitment by increments so small that none of them seemed to justify serious alarm.

If it proves to be the case that Soviet interest in the Middle East is indeed part of a global conception, this, too, would account for activity in all the countries and waters of the area. These would be complementary to Egypt and Syria in achieving a strategic advantage for the Soviet Union within the international system rather than solely on a regional basis. Thus, for example, each of the various ports and naval bases to be found in the region may be important in implementing a more assertive policy in the Third World.

Ideology, while perhaps subservient to power dictates and to Russian national interests, nevertheless enters into Soviet considerations. Each "progressive" revolution in the Arab Middle East, every trade agreement and cultural pact between the Soviet Union and

Middle Eastern countries and the visits to Moscow by Arab and Muslim dignitaries serve to vindicate the Cold War strategy of the Soviets to themselves as well as to their critics. In the face of attacks from Communist China that it has abandoned the class struggle against capitalism and has deviated from the militant doctrines of Marxism-Leninism, the Soviet leadership can point with some degree of pride to the gains achieved in the Middle East precisely because of peaceful coexistence. Having seized upon the theme of anti-imperialism, the Soviets may be captives of their own imagination by viewing support for even the least significant Arab country as a further blow against the West. Of course, the fact that the Soviet Union has projected an image of itself as the principal defender of the Arabs only makes it more difficult to withhold support from an Arab group which solicits the aid of Moscow.

Another explanation for the propensity of the Soviets to underwrite Arab causes lies in their drive to fill any void left by the British. The British may have begun their imperial experiences in the Middle East with modest designs for protecting India. But in the course of time their control of the key naval points of Constantinople, Egypt, Aden, and Basra dictated further interference in the internal affairs of the entire region. This, in turn, led to an expanded conception of the vital interests of the British Empire in order to protect the investment already made in Syria and Egypt. All of these characteristics of the British involvement—power politics, a broad strategic perspective, ideology, and a familiar dynamic of imperialism—are reflected in the Soviet effort.

Now with comprehensive interests and concerns in the Middle East, the Soviet Union must distinguish between vital and secondary aims. Guaranteeing one's national security, which is a fundamental principle of foreign policy, leads the category of legitimate objectives. Beyond this, the Soviet Union may work to establish a claim that the Middle East falls within its sphere of influence. In the coming years the Soviet Union may project itself as a major factor in the international oil sector, helping to regulate the flow, to establish the price, and to determine the markets for oil produced in the Middle East. Because of its naval presence, the Kremlin may even wish to emulate London by acting as guarantor of the freedom of the seas. At a minimum, it could ensure unimpeded transit for its warships and commercial vessels through the strategic passages of the region without being beholden to any other world power.

It would be far more difficult for the Soviets to go beyond acceptable bounds in order to pursue a manipulative policy in the Arab Middle East. Given the long, bitter struggle of the Arab people for independence, any renewed attempt at dominating them can only produce a repetition of the experience of previous imperial intruders, leading to animosity and resistance by the Arabs. But as long as the Soviets are able to maintain friendly relations with the Turks, the Iranians, and the Arabs by satisfying their needs, the only inherent limitation upon Russian primacy will come from within the Soviet society and government.

Thus far, success in the Middle East is owing to Soviet dedication of purpose, large outlays of funds, and the high priorities given to Arab friendship and to the naval component of the Soviet military. These policies could not be continued in the event of any internal power struggle, a shift in priorities, disillusionment with the policy of involvement in Middle Eastern affairs, or a major setback in the Arab world, such as the defection of a valued ally. A change in Soviet leadership or priority upon domestic consumption could also necessitate a revision in Middle Eastern policy in which strategic thinking might have to be modified and political activity curtailed. By establishing ties with the Arab countries and enlarging the Soviet commitment, the architects of foreign policy have raised the possibility of extending themselves beyond their earlier intentions and of living beyond their economic means. They shall have to give more attention henceforth to matching commitments with resources available for such purposes. Infusions of capital and military supplies on liberal terms to Arab clients is a heavy burden for the Russian economy; so is the construction of a large, modern, and balanced navy.

The Middle East has received a major share of Soviet economic and military aid. It has been estimated that of the $4 billion in military assistance dispersed from Moscow by the end of 1965, the United Arab Republic received approximately $1.5 billion, and Iraq and Syria more than $0.5 billion. Middle Eastern countries are also receiving about 40 percent of the Soviet economic assistance to developing countries.[1] Since 1954, Russian economic aid to the United Arab Republic alone has been more than $7.4 billion, while Eastern European countries added a further $5.4 billion. Arab losses of Soviet-supplied military equipment ran to an estimated $1 billion in the Six-Day War against Israel. By the end of 1968 the Russians were reported to have supplied an equivalent of that amount in replenishing the Arab arsenals and in restoring the armies of Egypt and Syria to their former state of readiness. How long the Soviets are prepared to incur such a level of expenditure is questionable.

A further challenge to the Soviet position in the Middle East lies in the realm of administration. The initial phase of penetration is nearing completion, and the second phase of entrenchment is already well under way. The Soviets shortly must enter (if they have not already done so) the third, and in many ways more difficult, phase: good management. They will have to protect the interests they have secured while, at the same time, determining whether a further increase of responsibilities will be necessary or even advantageous. In seeking to make firm and lasting the position they now hold, the Soviets might do well to heed the advice of a Russian chancellor in the early nineteenth century. Count Nesselrode suggested that a prudent policy requires "examining seriously the consequences for which we must be prepared; the sacrifices which Russia will have to make; the measures of precaution so that we may be ready, whatever may come, to support the dignity of Russia if it is compromised, to defend its safety if it is in danger."[2] Continued Soviet involvement in the Arab world will necessitate some clarification of interests and the establishment of priorities. The Arab countries, despite their strategic attractiveness, are certainly not comparable, either in terms of security or risks, to Czechoslovakia and the socialist commonwealth in Eastern Europe.

Tactical limitations have been cited as the second constraint on Soviet ambitions. Critics of the Soviet naval posture in the eastern Mediterranean, for example, point to such deficiencies as the lack of air cover and the vulnerability of supply lines. The Soviet squadron, despite its occasional deployment of fifty to sixty ships, is not comparable either in size or fire power to the Italian navy, let alone the Sixth Fleet or the combined naval strength of NATO.[3] As late as February, 1969,

British Defense Minister Denis Healey felt assured that, should a conflict occur, the Soviet navy in the Mediterranean "could be sunk in a matter of minutes."[4] These observations, if viewed in terms of an overt confrontation with the West, possess considerable validity. However, in terms of the present status of neither war nor peace, they may not reflect an adequate appreciation for the value of this naval presence and for its use in influencing the politics of smaller regional states.

Even in such an extreme situation as nuclear war, Soviet military planning may call for its regional allies to provide limited air cover and airbase facilities. The importance of Libya for such purposes has already been mentioned. In addition, Soviet planes with Egyptian markings have been sighted in aerial reconnaissance over the eastern Mediterranean, and Soviet pilots are included among the advisers stationed in Egypt. The Soviet Union is reported to have facilities at several Egyptian, Syrian, and Iraqi airfields; these would partially compensate for the conspicuous lack of aircraft carriers in the Soviet naval contingent in the Mediterranean. The Russians are also interest in securing overfly rights, landing privileges, and technical facilities from friendly Middle Eastern governments in order to remedy the handicap of extended supply lines.

The closure of the Suez Canal has placed perhaps an even greater limitation on Soviet strategic and tactical flexibility precisely because it does not lend itself to unilateral Soviet action. The canal became a part of the larger Arab-Israeli dispute in 1948. Its closure in 1956 and again in 1967 was a function of the conflict between Egypt and Israel, and its reopening can take place only after renewed conflict leaves Egypt victorious or Israel in control of the west bank of the canal. The third alternative is a negotiated settlement between the two countries. Short of any one of the three "extreme" alternatives, the enduring stalemate leaves the Suez Canal useless to all trading nations one hundred years after its inauguration.

The Soviet Union has been one of the nations most handicapped by the status quo since 1967 with regard to the Suez Canal, as seen in the Soviet inability to supply North Vietnam swiftly and efficiently.[5] Once again, as in the nineteenth century, the Russians are being deprived of the shortest strategic route to the Far East. The irony is that in earlier decades Russia's right to use this route was jeopardized by an admitted foe, Great Britain. At present, it is Egypt, the major Soviet client in the region, that contributes together with Israel to the closure. The dilemma for the Kremlin is whether to seek the canal's reopening by pressuring its ally to make diplomatic concessions against its will, and thus risk alienating Egypt, or by threatening Israel with force unless it withdraws from the east bank of the canal, and thus risk a direct confrontation with the United States. The single possible benefit from the closure is that the world's attention has been diverted from the canal area, enabling the Soviets to quietly expand their influence along both sides of the Red Sea.

Further restraints on long-range maritime ambitions arise from the continued Soviet dependency on Turkey for exit to the Mediterranean from the Black Sea. Ankara has consistently rejected Soviet insistence on a revision of the Montreux Convention. Given the existing détente in Soviet-Turkish relations, Moscow understandably prefers not to prejudice its position by renewing demands for a revision. On the other hand, the Soviets may view their good neighbor policy as making the Turks eventually amenable to such a revision. In any case, though relations with both Turkey and Iran presently are amicable, there is no Soviet guarantee of their remaining so. Old suspicions endure on both sides which could easily be aroused once again. If there were a recurrence of ill-feeling between the Soviet Union and either Turkey or Iran, or both, the Soviets would have to concentrate on policy closer to home. Avoidance of any such recurrence, with its implications for Soviet global flexibility and Middle Eastern policy, is thus one of the priorities as the Soviet Union shifts from penetration to management.

Success or failure for the Soviet Union in the Arab world, when viewed from the perspective of the 1970s, will surely lie in the delicate area of relations with the Arab people and their leaders. There is room for arguing that the actions initiated in the last fifteen years by President Nasser vis-à-vis Israel and against the West would have been done even without Russia's presence. What is important is that Soviet interest, indeed its mere existence as an alternative to the West, increased his chances of success. Equally important is that even though Soviet and Egyptian interests coincided in the past, there is less reason to expect this symmetry to continue. Soviet contacts with the other Arab leaders make them hesitate to share in Nasser's conception of Egyptian dominance over the Middle East. Intraregional pressures work to commit him ever deeper against Israel, whereas the existence of the latter is still acceptable to the Kremlin. The Russians, having looked to the region longingly for so many years, and having established a presence through considerable effort and expenditure in the past decade, may yet conclude that it is, after all, a dubious prize. Like their predecessors, the Russians' plans, whether grandiose or modest, may be frustrated by Arab contentiousness.

It is one thing to gain direct access to the Arab Middle East; it is an entirely different matter to retain whatever influence has been acquired and to exert it without alienating one's clients. As Britain, France, and even the United States have become aware, manipulative policies in this particular region usually have the defect of being overly clever. The British, despite their Lawrence of Arabia and H. St. John Philby types, failed because they did not recognize Arab nationalism as the salient political factor in the Middle East.

False or superficial perceptions of the Arabs will be one source of difficulties which the Soviets are likely to incur in dealing with the Middle East. Previously the Turk and the Persian had been the preoccupation of Russian statesmen. Little political or scholarly attention had ever been given to the Arabs, a subject people before 1917 and a backward people, whose economies had not even reached the capitalist stage of development, after the Russian Revolution. After the Second World War, when events presented an opening for the extension of influence, the Russians thrust themselves into the Arab world without adequate preparation or background information. This lack of understanding or sensitivity reflected itself in the Soviet failure and loss of prestige during the 1950s.

While the Soviets have been punctilious in expressing respect for Arab sovereignty, they show a proclivity for underestimating Arab intransigence in their pursuit of national interests. The consequence has been considerable responsibility in the Arab states without a commensurate degree of control. In May, 1967, the Syrians persuaded the Soviets that an Israeli attack was imminent despite the lack of conclusive evidence; the actual crisis thus was precipitated. Nor is it at all clear that the unilateral closure of the Straits of Tiran by President Nasser was fully coordinated with the Kremlin.[6] Russian judgment at that time was poor, and its intelligence network inept. The resultant military débâcle necessitated a Soviet reappraisal of its relationship with the progressive Arab states. Had the Soviet leaders desired to do so, they could have started de-emphasizing the relationship. Instead, partially because their identification with the Arabs was already too strong to allow defection, they increased military and diplomatic support. They still suffered from the traditional conception of alliances whereby the dominant party's proffering of vital aid necessitated obedience on the part of its dependent allies.

Since 1967, however, Soviet calculations have had to include the possibility of the Arabs acting independently in their "war of attrition" against Israel. Toward the end of 1969 there was growing Soviet verbal support for *al-Fatah* and associated Palestinian groups, behind which was the hope of gaining leverage over these least responsible and most independent of Arab organizations. The recurrence of a crisis situation at this time would imperil prospects for a further détente with the West, jeopardize peaceful Soviet gains in the Middle East, and, least desirable for the Soviet Union, involve it directly in a regional clash. These dangers, when added to the present frustration over the Suez Canal, ceaseless expenditure, vagaries of the oil market, and a strategic conception of the region always subject to review, could provide the basis at some future point for a decline in Soviet interest in the Middle East.

Meanwhile, their relationship with the Arabs poses three dilemmas for Soviet policy makers: arbitration, identification, and gratification. By befriending Arab states throughout the Middle East, the Soviets not only have made themselves privy to Middle Eastern affairs, as they desired, but to the many intraregional feuds as well. It will be increasingly difficult for the Soviet Union to remain a disinterested party whenever two of its clients are at odds.

While the Arab countries, except for the hard core of prowestern states, may agree on general systemic issues, such as the validity of socialism, anti-imperialism, and economic development, there is no such consensus on specific local issues. Thus, the Soviets must view as inopportune the rivalry between such personalities as President Nasser and the Shah of Iran. Similarly, the dispute over navigation rights in the Shatt al-Arab between Iraq and Iran, which reached the shooting stage in 1969, is an awkward one for Moscow, which is on friendly terms with both countries. Given the virtually limitless issues and areas for conflict in the contemporary Middle East, Prime Minister Kosygin's role at Tashkent in 1965 as arbiter of the India-Pakistan dispute with China may prove a useful precedent. In the context of the Middle East, the Soviet Union could work to resolve local differences, contain them, or else pursue its earlier course of exploiting local tensions by following the old imperialist policy of "divide et impera." Should they choose the first alternative of a mediatory capacity, the Soviets would fulfill a valuable function on behalf of the international community by contributing to local stabilization; at the same time it would conform to Soviet self-interest. Leaving regional disputes to fester runs counter to the Soviet need for cohesion among its Arab allies. Yet entering into the delicate field of arbitration opens the possibility for alienating one or more of these allies.

A second dilemma stems from the ascendancy of Yasir Arafat and the Palestinian liberation movement since 1967. In the past the Soviet government has been reluctant to endorse terrorist activity or to render support for it. Especially now that Moscow has secured itself in the region, its preference is for Egypt and its fellow "progressive" states to maintain a militant posture on international issues and, at the same time, to devote their energies to social and economic development rather than to regional adventures. Yet the Lebanese internal crisis in 1969 only confirmed the regional sway of Arafat and *al-Fatah* as advocates of extremism. They are free of any obligations to the Soviet Union; nor are they beholden to any Soviet regional client. The Soviets fear that withholding support for these groups only drives them further into the grasp of China, from which they derived the belief that victory can only be obtained at gunpoint. Arafat made a point of following up his visit to Moscow with a more publicized mission to Peking.

The dilemma, in short, is whether the Soviets will choose, or even be forced, to identify with the extremist elements in the Arab world, or whether they can preserve their gains by encouraging more moderate elements. Protecting investments and the politics of success induce a heightened degree of conservatism on the part of the imperial power. In this context, President Nasser, after eighteen years in power, began to resemble less of the revolutionary and more of the pragmatist when compared with the newer forces of Arab dogmatism and irresponsibility, such as *al-Fatah*. Nasser, the middle-aged president, perhaps chastened by past setbacks, is more reminiscent of Iraq's Nuri al-Said of the 1940s than of the young Colonel Nasser of the 1950s.

Long regarded as the symbol of Arab independence, President Nasser now finds his country compromised from several directions and his own latitude constricted. He has enabled an outside power to establish its presence and influence in Egypt and the Middle East. The prominence of *al-Fatah* necessitates his espousing radicalism for fear of losing his position as nominal leader of the Arabs. Owing to the serious loss of revenue from the Suez Canal, Egypt is financially dependent upon the largesse of Libya and the two reactionary monarchies of Kuwait and Saudi Arabia, which contribute over \$250 million annually to keep Egypt solvent. His contempt for the reactionary monarchies notwithstanding, Nasser provided asylum for two deposed rulers, King Saud and King Idris. President Nasser also adopted a moderate position during the Islamic Congress at Rabat and subsequently in mediating the Lebanese crisis. His reputation among Arabs and his survival are therefore very much in the Soviet interest—so long as he remains sensitive to the Soviet stake in avoiding a great power confrontation.

The third dilemma results from the Soviets acting as chief purveyor to the Arabs. Inherent in an alliance relationship are two dynamics: (1) the dominant ally will be valued only so long as its support is both needed and forthcoming and (2) the original superior-subordinate relationship with time will tend to balance itself, as the United States found in South Vietnam, as the client assumes a more assertive posture and escalates its demands. If the United States has to consider whether evenhandedness toward the Arabs leads ultimately to appeasement, so does the Soviet Union when it becomes a question of either resisting or appeasing Arab requests for multiple forms of "fraternal assistance and support."

The Soviets already find themselves in a relationship of interdependence with their Arab clients. In return for enabling the Soviets to claim influence, the Arabs expect Moscow to supply loans, weapons, technical advice, diplomatic support, and favorable terms of trade. The Arabs are likely to increase these expectations; already there is dissatisfaction at Soviet reluctance to supply more sophisticated weapons systems and offensive equipment such as ground-to-ground missiles. Moscow has not been anxious to go beyond the 1967 level of military hardware provided to Egypt and Syria; Cairo's pleas for MIG-23 fighters and more ground-to-air missiles were accepted only after Nasser personally flew to Moscow in January, 1970. In addition, Egyptian officers have found Russian equipment often unsuitable for the climatic conditions and desert terrain in that country. A further source of complaint in the past was the difficulty and delay in obtaining spare parts from Russia. The problem for the Soviets is essentially one of determining their ceiling of support for the Arabs, of satisfying the needs of clients without having them become so strong as to follow an independent course.

Should the Arabs lose again to Israel in a fourth round of open hostilities this would, of course, make them that much more dependent on the Soviet Union. For the same reason, the Kremlin is prepared to see Egypt suffer limited military setbacks. After a while, however, factions within the Soviet Union must begin to question the worth of such clients who perform poorly, take for granted continued Russian assistance, and threaten to force great power involvement. Conversely, if the Arabs achieved a victory over Israel, or if they should agree to negotiations on a pattern of those conducted at Rhodes in 1949, the grip of the outside power, Russia, would be reduced and the *raison d'être* of the Soviet-Arab alliance would be weakened. Lastly, if the Arabs embarked on an independent course against Israel, the Soviets, as in June, 1967, would be forced into a position of either protecting their interests at all costs or of seeing them sacrificed. In such an event, the Arabs will have assumed the aggressive role in the Soviet-Arab relationship.

Opportunities for friction, therefore, are almost limit-less. It will be difficult for the Soviets to avoid blurring the lines between supplying weapons, instructing how they are to be used, and, ultimately, dictating when they are to be used and against whom. It is in such sensitive policy areas that the question will be answered whether the Soviets are pursuing a policy of influence or of domi-nation over the Arabs. In either case, the Soviets will come to appreciate the subtleties between dependent and dependable allies.

By 1970 the vital alliance function of consultation was producing the first traces of friction—the result of different priorities and responsibilities by both parties to the relationship. Arab oil-producers were less than pleased at the prospect of the Soviet Union as a compet-itor for oil markets in Western Europe or, alternatively, as the "honest broker" of Middle East oil. The Syrians briefly courted the Chinese as an alternative to dictation from Moscow and to caution the Russians not to take them for granted. In May, 1969, the Syrian chief of staff, Lieutenant General Mustapha Tlass, visited Pe-king at the head of a military mission. He was photo-graphed brandishing the little red book of sayings by Mao Tse-tung, to the understandable consternation of the Kremlin.

Relations between Moscow and Cairo are in a special category due to Egypt's centrality for Soviet policy in the Arab Middle East. In the aftermath of the 1967 war, the Russian ambassador, Vinogradov, came to wield con-siderable influence in Cairo, leading some Egyptians to compare him unfavorably with Lord Cromer of the nine-teenth century. The Egyptian military, stung by the 1967 defeat, sensitive to matters of pride and prestige, have not relished taking instructions from Russian advisers. Missile fuses were kept under Russian control under the argument that Egyptian soldiers had not yet reached the standard of operations. Incidents have become so frequent that special joint conciliation committees, made up of equal numbers of Russian and Egyptian officers, have been established to sort out disputes. Nor have they particularly welcomed candid Soviet appraisals of the setback which stress the venality, dilettantism, and defeatism of the Egyptian "military bourgeoisie."[7] The deposition of Ali Sabry, a favorite of Moscow's, in September, 1969, together with the promotion of General Zadik to chief of staff, who, unlike his predecessors, was not trained in the Soviet Union, were two more signs of strained relations between Moscow and Cairo at the highest levels of government. At the end of November, 1969, the authoritative Egyptian newspaper *al-Ahram* hinted at U.A.R.-U.S.S.R. misunderstandings by acknowledging that certain circles were "trying to sow discord" between the two countries. At a lower level, Soviet technicians, advisers, military officers, and sailors on shore leave, despite their correct behavior, tend to alienate the local merchants by their sobriety and the population generally by their group exclusiveness. By the end of 1969, there were fresh signs of a willingness by the U.A.R. to improve relations with France and the United States in order to regain a degree of latitude in its foreign relations. The visit to Cairo in April, 1970, by Joseph Sisco, U.S. assistant secretary of state for Middle Eastern affairs, symbolized the potential for a renewed American dialogue with Egypt.

The history of the Middle East since 1945 is essentially characterized by a struggle for succession in a formerly French and British sphere. The struggle, however, is not limited to the United States and the Soviet Union. After centuries of such foreign domination, the inhabitants of the region are determined to be masters of their own future. Perhaps this dynamic will ensure that once again the ambitions of an outside power will be frustrated by the particularism endemic to the region. Optimism would be warranted if the Arabs realize before it is too late that aid of any kind from any source, whether capitalist or fraternally socialist, is never bestowed by disinterested parties and is never free of dissimulation. Further encouragement could be derived from an Arab perception of the liabilities inherent in being committed to one side in the Cold War. The Arabs might also ponder whether Soviet domination or the existence of Israel is ultimately the greatest threat to Arab independence.

The Soviet-Arab relationship is thus the interplay of domestic, regional, and global conflicts and alignments with inherent contradictions. The Russians aspire to a special status in the southern tier of the Arab Middle East. The Arabs strive for unity and freedom and have been under the mistaken impression that Soviet friendship can be exploited for such ends. The Soviets, for their part, emphasize the need for integration in this relationship, while the Arabs view it as the foundation for greater independence. The Soviet navy in the eastern Mediterranean may offer the Arab countries protection, but its presence also increases their intransigence, for example on the Israeli issue, where Soviet interests may be more inclined toward compromise. Repeated Egyptian warnings that war is inevitable in the 1970s must be disturbing to many Soviet officials, particularly when such statements come from a source as close to President Nasser as Muhammad Hassanain Heykal, editor of *al-Ahram*. Even while supplying and supporting the Arabs, Soviet spokesmen have consistently spoken in terms of working for a political settlement in the Middle East. At the same time, however, these same Soviet spokesmen have insisted that Moscow would not consent to any political solution which was unacceptable to the Arabs themselves. Meanwhile, the Russian military presence worked to the detriment of any peaceful resolution of the Arab-Israeli impasse; as Radio Baghdad boasted in January, 1968: "the Soviet Union, by its military maneuvers, by parading its missile strength, and by moving about its fleet units in the Mediterranean, has given the proof that it is not prepared to water down the Middle East question and to let the 5 June crisis go on and on without a just solution" to be defined by the Arabs.

The question with gravest implications for the future, therefore, is which side of the Soviet-Arab equation will be subordinated to the other. Will the Arabs manage to have the Soviet Union commit itself fully on their behalf? Or will the Soviets ultimately have to adopt even coercive measures in order to incorporate the region into their larger frame of reference? Because this fundamental question is still at issue and its answer of considerable magnitude, the United States, in its response to the challenge of a strong Soviet presence in the Middle East, could be decisive.

VI. THE UNITED STATES AND THE DYNAMICS OF COUNTERPOISE

In earlier periods of history, a Russian naval presence in the eastern Mediterranean, the Red Sea, and the Persian Gulf would have been regarded with undisguised alarm, especially if it were accompanied by an extension of political influence to the land mass between the seas. Even when the British system of imperial defense was at its zenith, Lord Curzon warned that a single Russian port in the Persian Gulf would constitute a "wanton rupture" of the status quo. In contrast, the western powers, in recent reactions to the deep Soviet penetration of the Arab Middle East, for the most part have been noteworthy more for their equanimity than a sense of urgency, more for the competition among themselves than for the coordination of efforts against the Russians. There is the tendency, for example, to minimize the implications of Soviet naval maneuvers and to deduce from Soviet willingness to discuss outstanding European and substantive issues a desire for some form of global détente including the Middle East. The United States, Britain, and France, reminiscent of their relationship during the Suez crisis, have either neglected or disdained to consult each other fully in order to present a united front vis-à-vis the Soviet Union.

To be sure, Moscow is free to exploit regional weaknesses in the Middle East, but at the same time it is vulnerable to them. This factor suggests that in the future Soviet policy will illustrate a greater degree of caution toward the Arab world. Beyond this, however, no automatic balancing mechanism is known to political scientists which might ensure that Soviet gains in the

Arab world do not lead to an actual transformation in global politics. In the light of two world wars there are few believers in the thesis that "if there exists an international order, it tends to be mechanically self-adjusting and self-rectifying. As soon as the equilibrium is disturbed at any one point, compensatory action automatically emerges in some other part of the system."[1] Pressure in one direction has always had to be contained through effective counterpressure; a positive act of will is needed on the part of all parties, or at least the most prominent among them, interested in maintaining an efficacious and stable distribution of power.

Until now, the Soviets have been preoccupied with securing a position, and consolidating it, beyond the northern tier. They have yet to make known their intentions in the region: How will they use the newly acquired status? Will it be for peaceful or aggressive purposes? Yet several broad possibilities and generalizations may already be distinguished.

The U.S.S.R. is certain to continue its previous policy of denying the Middle East to the western powers, for it has proved singularly effective in recent years. The British are withdrawing not only from east of Suez, but from west of Suez, too. The Libyan revolutionary government, with Moscow's encouragement, succeeded in forcing British personnel to depart in March, 1970; similar demands have been accepted by the United States. Whereas the contest for power in the Middle East formerly was regarded as one between the Soviets and the West, it is now essentially limited to the Soviets and the United States. Britain and France can only retain a symbolic presence or reassert a modest degree of influence among the Arabs. The four-power talks, with their attendant publicity, have offered the two former imperial powers a useful means for salvaging pride and for pursuing self-interests. But for all practical purposes Britain and France have been denied any major role in Middle Eastern affairs by the Arabs themselves, and in this the Arabs have the full support of Russia. The principal external counterweight to Soviet regional paramountcy is therefore the United States.

Denial of friends and allies to the West, but specifically to the United States, will be a cardinal tenet of Soviet policy in this third decade of the Cold War. Using its new vantage point of a direct presence, the Soviet Union will seek to reduce the number of pro-western states, and their regional influence, by questioning the ability of America to protect its clients. The Soviets may content themselves with neutralizing Iran, Turkey, Jordan, Kuwait, Morocco, Saudi Arabia, Lebanon, and Tunisia. Alternatively, having been encouraged by coups in the Sudan and Libya, they may settle for no less than an alignment with the socialist camp. A corollary of this policy of denial would be the imposition of restrictions, by the Soviets, or more likely by their Arab supporters with Soviet backing, on western access to oil, markets, ports, airfields, and narrow maritime passages of the Middle East.

The Soviet Union hopes to use the Middle East's assets, not only as a measure in the East-West power struggle, but also, in a more positive sense, to serve specific Russian and Eastern European interests. Neutralization, amity, an explicit client relationship, or ultimately, direct control all contribute to the defensive security and economic progress of the Russian homeland. They provide the opportunity for necessary oil imports to the Eastern bloc, favorable terms of trade, support in international forums, and greater strategic and mercantile flexibility in war or peace. Unless effectively countered, the Soviet policy of preemption will tend toward establishing the Middle East as a sphere of influence ringed by a credible naval military presence, such as nuclear submarines, to illustrate the deep Soviet commitment and resolve.

In general, most conceivable political objectives of the U.S.S.R. will be facilitated in some form by the demonstrative application of sea power. Naval capability allows Moscow to deliver the goods needed to attract, succor, and retain clients in the Middle East, Africa, and Asia. It also means that the Soviet Union will no longer be dependent upon the United States or Britain for its maritime connections; it demonstrates the sovereign right of the Russians to use the Mediterranean and other waters to guarantee their own unobstructed communication with the great ocean highways. As former Premier Khrushchev stated, peaceful coexistence is premised upon an "extensive and *absolutely unrestricted* international trade." With this in mind, the Soviets are beginning to possess what was lacking previously: a conspicuous capacity for intervention under the most varied conditions and the ability to transfer striking power with all necessary speed. The closure of the Suez Canal is the only handicap imposed on Soviet global mobility.

The use of naval strength is particularly effective in the Middle East, where the countries are easily accessible by water and where the people place a high value on symbolic gestures. Showing the red flag in itself can produce political benefits for the U.S.S.R., as periodic naval visits cannot but impress upon the local Arab populations the immediacy of Soviet strength in the region.

More active employment of the Soviet navy introduces an additional set of contingencies by providing a naval *point d'appui* in the Mediterranean. The Kremlin may assume a presumptive right of intervention in regional politics, acting to contain a local crisis in the event of renewed friction in Cyprus or Lebanon. By a timely show of force Moscow could frustrate an attempted coup against one of its protégés, intervene in a civil war on behalf of one faction, offer tactical assistance to an insurgency movement, or ensure the success of a revolution against any prowestern government in the Middle East and North Africa.

Implications of Soviet strategic flexibility are likely to be felt beyond the Arab world, extending to East-West relations and to the Soviet leadership of the socialist camp. The Soviet navy in the eastern Mediterranean, whatever its deficiencies, is already substantial enough to preclude any unilateral intervention by Washington in Arab affairs, such as occurred in 1958 when marines were landed in Lebanon. Within the larger context of the Soviet-American rivalry, Russian warships could be employed in harrassment exercises aimed at interfering with western shipping, supply lines, and communications.

Particularly susceptible are those countries dependent upon the sea for oil shipments from the Middle East. Great Britain imports approximately 55 percent of its oil from the region and France 41 percent, while Italy and Germany import an estimated 75 percent and 34 percent, respectively. However, the industrial country most vulnerable to an aggressive Soviet naval policy in the Indian Ocean is Japan, which receives 90 percent of its oil needs from the Persian Gulf area. Russian interference in the sale of Arab or Iranian oil or interdiction of tankers would deal the Japanese a severe blow. Lacking a strong naval component of their own, the Japanese regarded as an ominous precedent the failure of European maritime powers to act jointly in defending freedom of navigation during the 1967 crisis. By thus refuting the western monopoly of the sea, even beyond the

Mediterranean itself, the Soviet Union can weaken regional groupings endorsed by the United States, intimidate smaller powers, and cast doubts as to the value of western or American promises of support.

The Soviet navy has also become a valuable instrument in relations with the communist bloc. Russian freighters make a regular run to North Vietnam, which serves to stiffen resistance against the United States and to prove that Soviet friendship goes beyond mere rhetoric. In keeping with the Brezhnev Doctrine, sea power at the western extremity of the Mediterranean would be useful in protecting socialist gains. Rumania, Yugoslavia, and Albania, which have contributed to the strains of polycentrism in Eastern Europe, are open to intimidation. All three are vulnerable to attack from the sea: Rumania from the Black Sea and the other two countries from the Adriatic. Therefore, it is hardly surprising to find President Tito upon occasion expressing the desire to have the Mediterranean neutralized and demilitarized, with *both* superpowers withdrawing their fleets.[2] Albania occupies a unique position, for its defection to Communist China at the start of the 1960s deprived the Soviets of a submarine base at Valona—yet another factor prompting the Soviet Union to renew its efforts at gaining access to the eastern Mediterranean through the Arab world.

Ideological friction and the power rivalry with Communist China, which began to involve military encounters in 1969, adds an entirely new dimension. Peking has proved to be a disconcerting factor at times for the Soviets in the Arab world. The Chinese are sharp critics of Russia's political intentions, terming its identification as a Mediterranean country merely "a fig leaf for . . . expansion to the Middle East."[3] Secondly, they have sought to undermine Soviet influence by appealing to Arab extremists, urging the pursuit of uncompromising guerrilla revolution in the Maoist pattern of protracted "peoples war," and pledging aid to radical forces. Such policies cause the Kremlin to accuse Mao Tsetung and those Arabs identifying with him of sabotaging efforts at a peaceful political settlement of issues facing the region.[4] Great Britain always had to formulate Middle Eastern policy in terms of the threat from either Russia or France; Soviet considerations likewise extend to China as well as to the United States.

If a Sino-Soviet war should eventuate after inconclusive and unsatisfactory negotiations, the Soviets would need to surmount the traditional problems of (1) supporting large combat units in the Far East and (2) defending Vladivostok. Access to the Black Sea, the Mediterranean, and the Red Sea would facilitate military operations. One scenario might find the Red Navy in the China Seas, positioned to launch missile attacks against the major urban and industrial centers along the coast of China. Similarly, control of the sea route eastward would enable the Soviet Union to supply requisite personnel and matériel to its allies in Southeast Asia in the case of extended conflict with China in that theater.

Moscow has sought in the past year to advance the idea of an Asian collective security system pointedly directed against China. Such a ring of encirclement, extending from Japan to Burma and relying as well on India and Pakistan, would be enhanced by a strong naval capability; the Red Navy, in such an arrangement, would be comparable to the U.S. Sixth Fleet in NATO strategic planning. Peking, not unmindful of the relevance of Soviet entrenchment in the Middle East, has alerted its people to the danger of "U.S. imperialism and Soviet revisionism" launching a large-scale "war of aggression"; and the Chinese press has picked up the theme of Soviet gunboat diplomacy aimed at creating sea supremacy for a Russian "social-colonial empire."[5]

This wide range of military and political options against a variety of opponents, together with the intention of the Soviet Union to assert its "indisputable right" to be in the pivotal region of the Middle East, has significance for the international community as a whole. A leading American analyst of Cold War strategy observed at the end of the 1950s that "in a contest with the Sino-Soviet heartland for this Asian rimland we and our allies have the tremendous advantage of easy access to the sea and control of the sea, as well as a large number of naval and air bases encircling Eurasia and the technical capability of transporting great quantities of men and equipment to various points of the Sino-Soviet periphery."[6] In the transformation that has taken place since then, the United States no longer enjoys "control" of the seas, and its large number of naval and air bases has been reduced; indeed, of late it is the Soviet Union that seems to aspire to such a strategic advantage, whether against its capitalist opponents or communist rivals.

A key variable in considering the eventual importance of Soviet activity in the Arab Middle East, and whether this region will become the scene for sanguinary conflict or a peaceful field for trade, is the response of the United States. By the nature of its reaction, Washington can either constitute the most serious constraint on Russian ambitions or else encourage further Soviet expansion to the south and east.

In several ways the United States is unprepared to meet this challenge at the beginning of the 1970s. National temperament, fundamentally affected by the bitter experience of direct involvement in Southeast Asia, influences above all against any repetition of Vietnam. The American government and public, however divided over when and how to terminate their commitment in Vietnam, give the impression of being as one in desiring a more modest role in international relations. In seeking a definition of priorities, a great debate has been taking place between proponents of internal security and those favoring world security. Whether or not this portends a period of actual neo-isolationism, the United States is unlikely to involve itself in the Middle East if the Soviets do not mount a blatant challenge.

Another deterrent to U.S. involvement in the Middle East is that Americans quite clearly do not regard the area as fundamental to their interests. Oil represents the largest single interest the United States has there. Motivated more by financial profitability than by economy of savings, this interest has always centered on gaining valuable concessions to explore and produce the oil rather than on importing it for domestic purposes. Hence, part of the current dilemma is this marginal concern with a region regarded as vital by Western European allies and in which the Russians are demonstrating a primary interest. This disparity in attitudes is also seen in the comparatively low priority given to the Middle East in American foreign affairs except in times of crisis, as in 1956, 1958, and 1967.

If the United States is to counter Soviet advances, it is sorely in need of a stronger policy toward the Arabs. Though American leadership was sharply rebuffed in the 1950s, it was caused by President Nasser's and most Arabs' desire to pursue a policy of nonalignment in the spirit of the Bandung Conference of 1955; their motivation was not necessarily one of hostility toward the United States. At present, however, Arab sentiment is definitely anti-American and pro-Russian (though the two are not synonymous), the result not solely of U.S. identification with Israel but of a more fundamental insensitivity toward the Arabs. Any new policy designed to regain lost prestige must be premised on an endorsement of legitimate Arab aspirations, greater sensitivity to Arab nationalist feeling, an acceptance of other than democratic forms of government, and an awareness of the true sources for regional instability.

Time is obviously needed to rethink aspects of policy, including the basic question of whether Soviet paramountcy in the Arab Middle East is worth contesting from a global context. Other interim measures need not await clear answers. One significant response would involve an upgrading of sea power and naval strategy accompanied by further modernization of the American navy. Toward that end, Congress authorized $2.8 billion requested by the navy for fiscal 1970; plans call for the construction of sixty-two destroyers. The navy's esprit de corps in recent years has suffered from obsolescence and a series of embarrassments, including the loss of the *Scorpion*, damage to the *Liberty* in June, 1967, seizure of the *Pueblo*, and the collision of the *Evans* with an Australian ship in 1969.

One tangible step in filling the vacuum east of Suez would be an increase in American naval presence in the Persian Gulf, the Red Sea, and the Indian Ocean—waters which are not the immediate concern of either the Sixth Fleet or the Seventh Fleet in the Far East. Psychological benefits of showing the flag naturally are available to both sides; periodic cruises by U.S. warships in the Black Sea, for example, help to recall for the Soviets their own vulnerability close to home. U.S. ships in the Persian Gulf would be one direct means for reducing the chances of Soviet success after Britain's departure. An alternative, more desirable from the criteria of cost, involvement, and local sensitivities, would be diplomatic efforts to see to it that the local units—Iran, Saudi Arabia, Kuwait, and the sheikhdoms—cooperate so that they alone will fill the void at an early stage and preclude a great power contest.

Indications already exist of Washington's interest in several islands in the Indian Ocean that might serve as strategic naval and air bases in direct proximity to the Middle East; Diego Garcia has been selected as the site for an elaborate U.S. communications center. The ultimate advantage of naval power is that, unlike ground forces, it can be extricated with a minimum of difficulty if policy so dictates. For the present, however, small investments and an unmistakable show of resolve by the United States could dissuade the Soviet Union from pursuing a doctrine of paramount influence east of Suez and guarantee that the Russians do not proceed under any delusion about American intentions.

Washington's burden of leadership could be lightened considerably if defensive policy were to be actively coordinated with other nations. The list of countries affected by the Soviet initiative is fairly extensive: governments ranging from Yugoslavia to South Africa and from Tunisia to Japan are concerned, for example, about the possible implications for them of the Soviet navy in the Middle East. Their anxieties can be exploited and their individual resources mobilized through a common desire to provide a meaningful deterrent to Russian expansion. The European and Asian flanks of the Middle East constitute the two frameworks for a loose maritime coalition of intermediate and small powers.

If the acid test for any alliance is its being "a living thing, capable of growth, able to adapt to changing circumstances,"[7] then the Soviet maritime challenge is most opportune for NATO. It has caused the organization to address itself no less to developments in the eastern Mediterranean than to the familiar continental differences with Russia and Eastern Europe. In 1968, Maritime Air Command Mediterranean (MARAIR-MED) was created to keep a close watch on Russian naval activity in the area. On May 28, 1969, the NATO Defense Planning Committee issued a communiqué approving the establishment of a naval on-call force for the Mediterranean and requesting the NATO military authorities to prepare a program including exercises and port calls. Former President de Gaulle—his lack of enthusiasm for NATO, and his hope for a détente with the U.S.S.R. notwithstanding—acknowledged the need for Western European attention to the Soviet naval threat before his departure from the French political scene. The significance of Mediterranean affairs helps to explain U.S. tolerance for the authoritarian regime in Greece and also Washington's insistence upon reaching an accord with Spain in June, 1969, covering the major naval base at Rota.

In western Asia, such countries as Ceylon, India, Malaysia, Singapore, Indonesia, and Pakistan could provide a nucleus for some form of mutual defense in the Indian Ocean.[8] Japan, New Zealand, Australia, and South Africa have also expressed concern about the repercussions of Britain's withdrawal.

Japan, emphasizing the need to keep the seaway of the Malacca Straits open and to escort tankers bringing oil from the Middle East, has embarked on a program to strengthen its small but respectable Maritime Self-Defense Force. It has been reported that the United States, in return for consenting to have Okinawa and the Ryukyu islands revert to Japan in 1972, has obtained Tokyo's pledge to pick up a larger share of the Asian defense burden. In June, 1969, the four Commonwealth Pacific powers—Australia, Malaysia, New Zealand, and Singapore—made a major policy decision, announcing that they would maintain an armed posture in the region. It is their avowed intention to be the substitute for, rather than merely contributors to, the British military role in the Far East.[9] South Africa also plans to strengthen its sea defenses, including construction of a submarine base at Simonstown. Its rationale is that South Africa will be assured of a maritime defense capability of its own; at the same time it could contribute to protecting the cape route, made strategically important by the closure of the Suez Canal. Behind all of these efforts, individual and collective, Great Britain intends to retain a general capability to act as an emergency fire brigade, able to return east of Suez in the event of local hostilities, albeit without any automatic commitment to intervene.

The Soviet effort may actually generate a new sense of cohesion in the ranks of the West by reactivating NATO and the other regional defensive systems. From the perspective of Asia and Africa, the broad Soviet offensive is perhaps more in the nature of a long-term threat to their economic and political independence. For the Arabs, however, current Soviet policy, if sustained, suggests that their resolve to never again become subservient to outside powers is facing its severest test.

In terms of American policy, the very fact of Moscow's military and political entrenchment in the Arab Middle East has put the United States on the defensive, forcing it to assume the risks connected with making a countermove. The transition in Soviet strategic thinking may or may not be part of an over-all communist design of total victory in the struggle against the United States and other free world nations. More likely, it can be explained in terms of the standards expected of a great power in a state system characterized by rivalry and uncertainty: "Keep all you have and try for all you can," as it was once stated by Bulwer-Lytton. Nor is it necessarily true that "to contemplate a loss of U.S. naval supremacy is to contemplate disaster on an epochal scale."[10] But in all planning and analysis American strategists and diplomats will have to account for the Soviet strategic mobility and for Soviet influence with the Arabs. Russian ascendancy implies that in the decade of the 1960s the Soviets directly refuted any notions of American pre-eminence in world affairs; rather than accepting any diminution, they give every indication of maintaining or even enhancing their superpower status.

Under these conditions, an effective American riposte might consist of at least three fundamental, interrelated phases. The first, as already mentioned, requires a determination of whether Soviet primacy in the southern tier is worth contesting. If so, then the United States must fashion a diplomatic and military policy of its own in the Middle East, aimed at disengaging the Arabs from the Soviet Union. Should this be sought at the price of Israel, the United States runs the double risk of alienating one confirmed ally without any guarantee of winning over the Arabs to its side. Initial reactions both by the Arab states and by Israel to Secretary of State William Rogers' speech of December 9, 1969, seemed to confirm this likelihood. If this happened American isolation would be more pronounced than at any time since 1967.

The second phase would be to force the current Russian advance to a standstill. It entails bringing sufficient power and influence to bear in order to increase the strains under which Soviet policy must operate. The Kremlin would thereby find it necessary to exercise a far greater degree of moderation and circumspection. As originally formulated by George Kennan and others, the essence of an enduring Cold War is the adroit and vigilant application of counterforce by the free world to a series of constantly shifting geographical and political points corresponding to the shifts and maneuvers of Soviet policy. Their premise, endorsed by successive American administrations, was that if the Kremlin found unassailable barriers in its path, it would accept these philosophically and accommodate itself to them. The northern tier land barriers having proved quite assailable, the United States must now take up a new defensive position along the waterways comprising the southern tier of western Asia. Greater appreciation for the Middle East's importance in present international conditions expressed in a more dynamic policy and strengthened naval presence, together with the collaboration of other interested parties, might represent the essential features of this new American position.

A fresh approach and the containment of the Russian thrust would enable the United States to engage in the third and most important phase: striving for an accommodation with the Soviets in an era of negotiation. On the assumption that their political-military program in the Middle East is not a bold attempt at uncompromising hegemony, and indeed to discourage any such pretensions, the United States should encourage common approaches where interests converge: ensuring freedom of the seas for all nations and navigation through narrow sea passages; prohibiting use of the seabed and ocean floor for other than peaceful purposes; limiting both the quantity and quality of arms supplied to Middle Eastern countries; and taking joint action to contain local flareups.

Both superpowers have learned from previous involvements in Middle Eastern affairs to appreciate the dangers implicit in the region; if nothing else, the 1967 crisis made this point clear. Operating from this realistic foundation, and aware that true political stability cannot be imposed, the United States and the Soviet Union could work instead toward the solution of regional ills through economic development and a strengthening of the Arab social fabric.

For the Soviet Union, this would entail a shift of emphasis, because of its tradition since 1945 of exploiting the social malaise of the Arab societies. Nevertheless, the ideal of cooperation tests the maturity of the Soviet Union as a responsible global power able to practice self-restraint in the conduct of foreign policy.

For the United States, such an accommodation would in several ways be no less difficult. It means accepting the fact that western political primacy in the Arab world has ended. It further challenges the United States to accept condominium and a rough parity in the Mediterranean, with all of the tension and room for cooperation that the concept implies. Above all, the pursuit of cooperation requires of the United States that it view recent Soviet penetration of Middle Eastern lands and waters from a Russian historical perspective: as compensatory rather than imbalancing.[11] Hereafter, the challenge for American diplomacy and military preparedness in playing a compensatory role will be not to exclude the Soviets from the Mediterranean or the Arab world, but to ensure no less for the free world than equal rights and privileges of access, passage, trade, and contact. This arrangement would welcome Russia's triumph over history and geography while safeguarding American national and international interests.

What remains unclear at the outset of the 1970s is whether the United States and the Soviet Union can actually permit themselves to be guided by long-range interests, and not merely by temporary political considerations, in their approaches to the Arab Middle East. Is the United States prepared to adopt a policy of accommodation which demands vigilance and initiative without any prospect of victory? And is Soviet Russia, released at last from its old geographical confines, in the ascendant and tasting the first fruits of success, willing to settle for any status short of paramountcy?

The decade of the 1960s, in any case, ended rather inconclusively for most of those regional and extra-regional parties involved in fashioning Middle Eastern politics.

The Soviet Union, which has contributed so much to the discomfiture of all these parties, on the surface would seem to have the most cause for satisfaction as the 1970s begin. Still, it cannot view with equanimity the instability of its Arab clients or their friction with each other. Many of its new and evolving interests in the region depend on the "strengthening of unity of Arab countries and peoples, their cohesion and cooperation with all the anti-imperialist forces," as President Nikolai Podgorny and Premier Alexei Kosygin stressed in their joint message of greeting to the Arab Summit meeting in Rabat toward the end of 1969.

The striking absence of any common ground thus far between the regional members, the former imperial countries, or the present superpowers only increases the chance of the various Middle Eastern tensions exploding in greater intensity and over a greater radius.

The United States and the Soviet Union, in joint author-
ship whether through collaboration or discord, and
with contributions by the Arabs, Turks, Persians, and
Israelis, are therefore fated to write the newest chapter
of the Eastern Question during this decade.

NOTES

Chapter I

1. See, for example, General L. L. Lemnitzer, "The Strategic Problems of NATO's Northern and Southern Flanks," *Orbis*, vol. 13, no. 1 (Spring, 1969), pp. 100–10. Studies on the Soviet initiative thus far have not analyzed it as a comprehensive effort; rather, they have stressed its implications in a single limited region. Examples are: Curt Gasteyger, *Conflict and Tension in the Mediterranean*, Adelphi Papers, no. 51 (September, 1968); and J. B. Millar, *The Indian and Pacific Oceans: Some Strategic Considerations*, Adelphi Papers, no. 57 (May, 1969), both published by the Institute for Strategic Studies in London.
2. Sir John A. R. Marriott, *The Eastern Question. An Historical Study in European Diplomacy*, 4th ed. (Oxford: The Clarendon Press, 1940), p. 39.

Chapter II

1. *Bombay Courier*, March 25, 1826, quoted in Halford Hoskins, *British Routes to India* (London: Frank Cass & Co., Ltd., 1928), p. 105.
2. *British Interests in the Mediterranean and Middle East* (Report by a Chatham House Study Group for the Royal Institute of International Affairs; London: Oxford University Press, 1958), p. 81.
3. Many of the lost opportunities and miscalculations in U.S. policy toward the Nasser regime in the years of its infancy are described in Miles Copeland, *The Game of Nations* (London: Weidenfeld and Nicolson, 1969). According to Copeland, and contrary to the usual interpretation, Israel was not the irritant in American-Egyptian relations during the 1950s.
4. *New York Times*, September 27, 1968.
5. Merle Fainsod, "Some Reflections on Soviet-American Relations," *The American Political Science Review*, Vol. 62, no. 4 (December, 1968), pp. 1093–103.
6. "A Talk with President Nasser," *Newsweek*, February 10, 1969, p. 36.

Chapter III

1. See Philip E. Mosely, *Russian Diplomacy and the Opening of the Eastern Question in 1838 and 1839* (Cambridge: Harvard University Press, 1934).
2. For a study of this phase of the Russian push southward, see Firuz Kazemzadeh, *Russia and Britain in Persia, 1864–1914* (New York: Yale University Press, 1968).
3. Text of "Draft, Secret Protocol No. 1," November, 1940, in Ralph H. Magnus, ed., *Documents on the Middle East* (Washington: American Enterprise Institute for Public Policy Research, 1969), p. 55.
4. A pioneering study on Soviet attitudes toward the Arab world emphasizing the interplay between ideology and the Russian national interest is found in Walter Z. Laqueur, *The Soviet Union and the Middle East* (New York: Frederick A. Praeger, 1959).
5. V. Rumyantsev, "The U.A.R.: The Struggle Continues," *Pravda,* June 6, 1969.

Chapter IV

1. "Tripartite Declaration on Security in the Arab-Israel Zone," May 25, 1950, in J. C. Hurewitz, *Diplomacy in the Near and Middle East. A Documentary Record: 1914–1956* (Princeton: D. Van Nostrand, 1956), Vol. 2, pp. 308–9.
2. See Geoffrey Kemp, "Strategy and Arms Levels, 1945–1967," in J. C. Hurewitz, ed., *Soviet–American Rivalry in the Middle East* (New York: The Academy of Political Science, 1969), p. 24. The changing pattern of suppliers is reflected in the steadily rising number of jet aircraft, tanks, and warships delivered by the Soviet Union to Algeria, Egypt, Iraq, Morocco, and Syria. This trend accelerated after 1967 and is likely to be reinforced by requests from Libya, the Sudan, and Southern Yemen.
3. Herbert Feis, *The Birth of Israel* (New York: W. W. Norton & Company, 1969), p. 51.
4. Cf. Henry A. Kissinger, *Nuclear Weapons and Foreign Policy* (New York: Council on Foreign Relations, 1957); and Robert E. Osgood, *Limited War: The Challenge to American Strategy* (Chicago: University of Chicago Press, 1957).
5. Herbert S. Dinerstein, "The Revolution in Soviet Strategic Thinking," *Foreign Affairs,* vol. 36, no. 2 (January, 1958), pp. 241–52, describes the reappraisal which followed Stalin's death. See also Thomas W. Wolfe, "Russia's Forces Go Mobile," *Interplay,* March, 1968, pp. 28–37.

6. Marshal V. D. Sokolovsky, ed., *Military Strategy* (New York: Frederick A. Praeger, 1963).

7. Joseph J. Baritz, "The Soviet Strategy of Flexible Response," in Institute for the Study of the U.S.S.R., *Bulletin*, vol. 16, no. 4 (April, 1969), pp. 25–35. Also incisive is an article by Admiral of the Fleet Sergei G. Gorshkov, commander in chief of the navy of the U.S.S.R., "The Development of Soviet Naval Science," *Naval War College Review*, February, 1969, pp. 30–42. See also Commander Robert B. Rogers, "Trends in Soviet Naval Strategy," *Ibid.*, pp. 13–29.

8. Marshal Sokolovsky, though giving priority to nuclear strength, acknowledged that the main aims of naval operations would be to defeat the enemy fleet and disrupt his naval and sea communications. Missile strikes, support for ground troops, freight, and protection for Russian naval lines would also be expected to assume greater importance. *Military Strategy*, p. 298.

9. *The Military Balance, 1969–1970* (London: Institute for Strategic Studies, 1969), pp. 8–9.

10. *Voprosy istorii KPSS*, 1967, p. 113.

11. R. Andreasyan, "Revolutionary Democrats of Asia and Africa," *Aziya i Afrika Segodnya*, no. 10 (1966), p. 5. See also excerpts from the principal document adopted by the world conference of communist parties in the *New York Times*, June 19, 1969.

12. *Ibid.*, June 20, 1967, pp. 16–17.

13. Petr Kruzhin, "The Soviet Fleet in the Mediterranean," in Institute for the Study of the U.S.S.R., *Bulletin*, vol. 16, no. 2 (February, 1969), pp. 35–37.

14. *Ibid.* Kruzhin also describes the composition of the Soviet squadron in the eastern Mediterranean.

15. *The Military Balance, 1968–1969* (London: Institute for Strategic Studies, 1968), pp. 7–8, 30, 52. See also the *New York Times,* August 21, 1969.

16. *Ibid.*, March 26 and 29, April 5, 1969.

17. TASS, May 23, 1967. Italics mine. Equally reflective of this new Soviet assertiveness are: L. Kolosov, "Mediterranean Problems," *Izvestia*, November 12, 1968; Vice Admiral Smirnov in *Red Star*, November 12, 1968. See also the *New York Times*, November 28, 1968.

18. *Pravda*, November 24, 1968.

19. Nikolai Polyanov, *Izvestia*, May 26, 1969.

20. Charles Tugendhat, *Oil: The Biggest Business* (London: Eyre and Spottiswoode, 1968), p. 225.

21. As evidenced in Nasser's speech before the Egyptian National Assembly on November 7, 1969, condemning the United States and praising the Soviet Union, which "stands besides us inter-

nationally and provides us with arms." The growth in Soviet–
Egyptian relations between 1955 and 1967 is described in detail
by Charles B. McLane, "Foreign Aid in Soviet Third World
Policies," *Mizan*, vol. 10, no. 6 (November–December, 1968).
22. See, for example, Robert E. Hunter, "Oil and the Persian
Gulf," *The Soviet Dilemma in the Middle East*, Adelphi Papers,
no. 60 (London: Institute for Strategic Studies: October, 1969),
pp. 2–5; Lincoln Landis, "Soviet Interest in Middle East Oils,"
The New Middle East, no. 3 (December, 1968), pp. 16–20; and
D. C. Watt, "Russians Need Middle East Oil," *Ibid.*, pp. 21–23.
23. *New Outlook*, vol. 12, no. 9 (November–December, 1969),
p. 62.

Chapter V

1. Franklin D. Holzman, "Soviet Trade and Aid Policies," in
Hurewitz, *Soviet–American Rivalry*, pp. 104–20; and a report by
Mr. Griffiths, rapporteur of the Western European Union's General Affairs Committee, in *NATO Newsletter*, June, 1969, pp.
4–5. He noted that in the period 1955–67, Egypt received $2 bil-
lion worth of Soviet military and economic aid, while Iraq,
Syria, and Algeria together received an additional $1.1 billion.
2. Nesselrode to Tsar Nicholas I, January, 1838. Cited in Mosely,
Russian Diplomacy, p. 17.
3. See, for example, Gasteyger, *Conflict and Tension*, pp. 44–45.
4. *The Economist*, February 15, 1969, quoting an interview
in *Der Spiegel*.
5. An abiding Soviet interest in the canal, despite its political
vulnerability, is expressed by George Mirsky in "The Soviet
View," *The New Middle East*, January, 1969, pp. 16–18. Resto-
ration of the canal would still enable supertankers to advance
up the Red Sea as far as Suez, from where oil could still be
pumped relatively cheaply to Alexandria.
6. The Soviet role in the 1967 crisis is considered by Walter Z.
Laqueur, *The Road to War, 1967* (London: Weidenfeld and
Nicolson, 1968), pp. 76–80, 178; and by Nadav Safran, *From
War to War: The Arab–Israel Confrontation, 1948–1967* (New
York: Pegasus, 1969), pp. 276–95.
7. A particularly scathing analysis was provided by Igor Belyayev and Yevgeny Primakov, "When War Stands at the Thresh-
old: Soviet Journalists Describe the Situation and Mood in the
U.A.R. After the Israeli Aggression," *Za rubezhom*, no. 27
(June 30–July 6, 1967) pp. 7–8. Belyayev expanded on this
thesis in *Pravda* on August 27, 1969, citing the faithlessness of
"the wheeler-dealers in generals' and colonels' uniforms," p. 4.

Chapter VI

1. Herbert Butterfield, *Christianity, Diplomacy, and War* (New York: Abingdon–Cokesbury, n.d.), pp. 89–90.

2. An indication of Yugoslav concern at growing Soviet naval strength in the Mediterranean is found in the authoritative newspaper, *Borba*, on May 24, 1969. President Tito again spoke out on this sensitive subject during his visit to Algeria in November, 1969.

3. "Soviet Revisionist Social Imperialism's Expansionist Activities on the Seas," *The People's Daily*, May 18, 1969.

4. Russian radio broadcast in Mandarin to China, May 24, 1969, after a Syrian military delegation had concluded its visit to Peking.

5. Excerpts from Deputy Chairman Lin Piao's report to the Ninth Congress of the Chinese Communist Party. *New York Times*, April 29, 1969.

6. Osgood, *Limited War*, p. 246.

7. President Nixon in an address before the Council of the North Atlantic Treaty Organization on February 24, 1969.

8. Already in 1960 Ayub Khan foresaw "the inexorable push of the north" in the direction of the Indian Ocean aided by regional squabbling on the subcontinent. "Pakistan Perspectives," *Foreign Affairs*, vol. 38, no. 4 (July, 1960), pp. 546–56. Present aspects are analyzed by J. B. Millar, *The Indian and Pacific Oceans: Some Strategic Considerations*, Adelphi Papers, no. 57 (London: Institute for Strategic Studies, May, 1969); Albert Axelbank, "Maritime Self-Defence." *Far Eastern Economic Review*, February 27, 1969; and *The Christian Science Monitor*, June 11, 1969, p. 13.

9. *New York Times*, June 20, 1969.

10. U.S. Congress, House, Committee on Armed Services, *The Changing Strategic Naval Balance, U.S.S.R. vs. U.S.A.*, 90th Cong., 2d sess., December, 1968, pp. 6, 12.

11. Vice-Admiral N. Smirnov, "A Black Sea, Hence Mediterranean Power," *Krasnaya zvezda*, November 12, 1968, p. 3.

Campbell, John C. *Defense of the Middle East*. New York: Frederick A. Praeger, 1960.

The Center for Strategic and International Studies. *Soviet Sea Power*. Special Report Series, no 10. Washington, D.C.: Georgetown University, June, 1969.

Herrick, Robert W. *Soviet Naval Strategy: Fifty Years of Theory and Practice*. Annapolis: U.S. Naval Institute, 1968.

Hoskins, Halford. *British Routes to India*. London: Longmans, Green, 1928.

Hurewitz, J. C. *Diplomacy in the Near and Middle East*. 2 vols. Princeton: D. Van Nostrand, 1956.

————. ed. "Soviet-American Rivalry in the Middle East." *Proceedings of the Academy of Political Science*, vol. 29, no. 3. New York: Columbia University, 1969.

Kerner, Robert J. *The Urge to the Sea. The Course of Russian History*. Los Angeles: University of California Press, 1942.

Laqueur, Walter Z. *The Soviet Union and the Middle East*. New York: Frederick A. Praeger, 1959.

————. *The Struggle for the Middle East*. London: Routledge & Kegan Paul, 1969.

Lewis, Bernard. *The Middle East and the West*. Bloomington: Indiana University Press, 1964.

Mahan, Alfred T. *The Influence of Sea Power Upon History*. Boston: Little, Brown & Company, 1890.

Marriott, Sir John A. R. *The Eastern Question. An Historical Study in European Diplomacy*. 4th ed. Oxford: The Clarendon Press, 1940.

Reitzel, William. *The Mediterranean. Its Role in America's Foreign Policy*. New York: Harcourt, Brace and Company, 1948.

The Royal Institute of International Affairs. *Political and Strategic Interests of the United Kingdom*. London: Oxford University Press, 1939.

Sokolovsky, Marshal V. D., ed. *Military Strategy: Soviet Doctrine and Concepts*. New York: Frederick A. Praeger, 1963.

Spector, Ivar. *The Soviet Union and the Muslim World, 1917–1958*. Seattle: University of Washington Press, 1959.